WITHDRAWN

HARVARD LIBRARY

WITHDRAWN

MORALITY AND AGENCY

by

Robyn McPhail
and
David E. Ward

UNIVERSITY
PRESS OF
AMERICA

Lanham • New York • London

Copyright © 1988 by

University Press of America,® Inc.

4720 Boston Way
Lanham, MD 20706

3 Henrietta Street
London WC2E 8LU England

All rights reserved

Printed in the United States of America

British Cataloging in Publication Information Available

Library of Congress Cataloging-in-Publication Data

McPhail, Robyn, 1954–
Morality and agency / by Robyn McPhail and David E. Ward.
p. cm.
Includes bibliographical references and index.
1. Agent (Philosophy) 2. Ethics. I. Ward, David E., 1940–
II. Title.
BJ1031.M34   1988
170—dc 19   88–10336 CIP
ISBN 0–8191–6980–3 (alk. paper)
ISBN 0–8191–6981–1 (pbk. : alk. paper)

All University Press of America books are produced on acid-free
paper which exceeds the minimum standards set by the National
Historical Publications and Records Commission.

For Elizabeth and Sheila

- D.W.

For Neil, Jeremy and Kim

-R. M.

ACKNOWLEDGMENTS

We would like to thank our colleagues within the Philosophy Department of the University of Otago, in particular Roy Perrett, for their willingness to read the manuscript and offer suggestions. We would also like to thank Sheila Ward, Margaret Higgins, Martin Frické and Bryan Wilson for proof-reading the manuscript; Anita Wells for her help in formatting the final draft; Peter Leech for proof-reading the final draft; our families for their patient support and especially two little boys who tried so hard to play quietly while Mama was doing "her work".

CONTENTS

Preface		ix
Abbreviations		xi
Introduction		xiii
Chapter One	Two Kinds of Value	1
Chapter Two	Kant's Shadow Model of Moral Causality	17
Chapter Three	Reflexive Decision-Making	35
Chapter Four	Groundwork for a transition to Spinoza	63
Chapter Five	Spinoza's Account of Human Agency	69
Chapter Six	Agency in Kant	83
Chapter Seven	Explaining Away the Evidence for Morality as a Form of Life	91
Chapter Eight	The Unique Viability of the Moral Form of Life	147
Index		159

PREFACE

In 1978 we joined forces as doctoral student and supervisor in a venture which converged on a comparison between the ethical systems of Immanuel Kant and Benedict Spinoza. During the three years in which we worked together we talked through a number of issues which went well beyond the scope of the submitted thesis.[1] When in 1981 the degree was granted, we both felt that it would be worth our while to continue to develop those ideas and this book is the result.

Kant and Spinoza are not often spoken of in the same breath and this is perhaps not surprising. Spinoza is regarded as a unique figure in the history of philosophy and is usually studied in isolation from the main stream of philosophers who have concerned themselves with ethics and moral theory. This is understandable given the fact that Spinoza's views on ethics are deeply embedded in a complex metaphysical system.

Here we will not be dealing with Spinoza's work in its metaphysical complexity but only with a few of his central ideas concerning agency which provide a solution to problems encountered within the moral form of life which Kant analysed so carefully. We begin with a practical concern dear to the hearts of all human agents—how to relate goodness and happiness, moral value and utility value. We then consult Kant and Spinoza whose opposed views on this topic allow us to illustrate the vital connection which exists between morality and agency.

---

[1] 'Kant's Antinomy of Practical Reason', By Robyn McPhail, unpublished Ph.D. thesis, University of Otago, Dunedin, New Zealand.

ABBREVIATIONS

Reference to works by Immanuel Kant and Benedict de Spinoza will be made throughout by means of a system of abbreviations. Reference to the Kantian texts will include a title in initials, paging of the selected English translation and the paging of the original German as given in the Insel-Verlag edition, Frankfurt, 1964. The English translations used are:

Critique of Pure Reason, translated by Norman Kemp Smith, Macmillan, London, 1929. Given as *CPR*.

Critique of Practical Reason and Other writings in Moral Philosophy, translated by Lewis White Beck, University of Chicago Press, Chicago, 1949. Given as *CPrR*. (This volume contains 'Foundations of a Metaphysic of Morals' (Given as *FMM*), 'Perpetual Peace: A Philosophical Sketch' and 'On a Supposed Right To Lie From Altruistic Motives')

Critique of Judgement, translated by J. C. Meredith, Clarendon Press, Oxford, 1952. This volume contains the 'Critique of Aesthetic Judgement' and the 'Critique of Teleological Judgement'. Given as *CJ*, CaJ/CtJ.

The Doctrine of Value: Part II of the Metaphysics of Morals, translated by Mary J. Gregor, Harper and Row, New York, 1964. Given as *MM*.

Religion Within the Limits of Reason Alone, translated by Theodore M. Greene and Hoyt H. Hudson, New York, 1960. Given as *RWL*.

Reference will also be made to Spinoza's *Ethics* to be found in *The Chief Works of Benedict de Spinoza Vol. II*, translated by R. H. M. Elwes, Dover Publications, New York, 1955. The form will be to cite the Elwes paging and then the sectioning of the original Latin in Books, Propositions, etc.

INTRODUCTION

To think that one ought to do something implies that one regards oneself as capable of doing the thing in question: morality implies (without, it seems, any hesitation) a certain conception of agency. Although this is a familiar implication it raises a problem: are we to accept that the existence of a moral form of life implies that people are *actually* capable of behaving morally? (This is what Kant thought.) Or must we first establish the scope and limits of human agency (a determination of what, in fact, we *can* do) in order to understand what 'ought' is to mean and therefore what force moral injunctions should be regarded as having?

There are two traditions which reflect these alternatives. The first finds its clearest exponent in Kant. For Kant, the voice of Duty speaks to an agent who must be thought of as possessing a free will in order to be regarded as capable of obeying Duty's call. That human agents are free is a postulate of morality as Kant understands it. It is only on the assumption of freedom that morality makes any sense. So for Kant it is the status of morality *as an established form of life* that leads him to assume a conception of human agency which is in tune with the requirements of morality.

Now the other tradition is not so easily identified with a single individual. No one has found it to be a straightforward business to set down exactly what a human being's powers are. The very fact that an agreed-upon description of our powers is not available is disconcerting: if human agents are not free, then it would seem to follow that their behaviour must be determined by various factors. But what exactly are these determinants and to what extent can they be discovered and understood? (Perhaps the source of the difficulty lies in the fact that the very act of identifying the determinants of human behaviour seems to rob them of their power as determinants thereby revealing another deeper aspect of our agency which requires a new description of its inner workings if human agency is to be properly understood, and so on, *ad infinitum*.)

However there is a further complication in this enterprise: what is the point of seeking out these determinants of human behaviour? It is clearly not just a matter of intellectual curiosity. Searching for a natural account of human agency is motivated by a desire to identify and thus assume control over the forces which account for the character of our behaviour. Our motives in this particular branch of natural history are decidedly ulterior. Any such enquiry serves (through a determination of the scope and limits of our control over our behaviour) to establish what standards of behaviour we can (and therefore ought) to expect from everyone, with consequences that affect every area of our lives. Since this constitutes *the* question for human agents there are plenty of answers to it. But the crucial fact about this whole enterprise is its more or less hidden assumption about our powers as agents: even though it is the premise of this enquiry into the nature of human agency that we are not free, nevertheless the motive of the enquiry springs from the belief that we can (freely?) control/manipulate the mechanisms of our nature once we discover them. Clearly there is nothing deterministic about this belief.

In fact, then, because an enquiry into our nature as agents is premissed on the belief that we could control ourselves if we but knew how, it follows that we intuitively regard ourselves as more or less in control of our agency. We already act as if there were powers within ourselves over which we have varying degrees of control. Unless we had this idea intuitively, the idea that we could control ourselves better if we knew more about how we 'work' could not get off the ground, and the motivation to search for such 'springs of action' would be absent.

Spinoza is the great advocate of the idea that it makes sense neither to speak of our control over ourselves as absolute (i.e. that we are free) nor to think that we have no control over ourselves (i.e. that we are determined). Since in his view our agency is neither free nor determined it must be understood by means of a different concept altogether. This third possibility is what we have described in this book under the term 'agent-naturalism'.

Such a 'compromise' notion is perhaps best understood by noting that human agents are *finite* agents. As finite, an agent is neither entirely free nor entirely determined. An agent is instead more or less active, more or less in control, more or less free.

Spinoza is the philosopher who, in our view, solves the problem of human agency by recognizing its *sui generis* status. He recognizes that it is neither a 'mechanical' (determined) phenomenon, nor a 'supernatural' (free) one, but instead something that must be understood on its own terms if it is to be understood at all. Thus we think it fair (if unfalsifiable) to say that those who understand Spinoza's conception of agency are convinced that he has got it right. (He himself was certainly of this opinion.)

However, despite 'the fact' that he was right, he remains an inaccessible[1] thinker. After all, if human agency is a hard thing to understand, then the theory which accurately captures its essence is also going to be hard to understand. At this point an infinite regress seems to loom, punctuated now and then by cries in the wilderness from those who have understood the master. This volume is not another such cry.

Our advocacy of Spinoza's views on agency is based on an independent investigation of the dialectic that links the concepts of morality and agency. This dialectic is reflected in (and itself reflects) the complex phenomenology of the moral form of life as it is integrated with our experience of our agency—our consciousness of ourselves as agents. It is then our exploration of this relationship which forms the main part of the book and serves as an indirect argument to the conclusion that Spinoza was right about the nature of human agency.

The motive for this exploration derives from our fascination with the 'romance' of Kantian morality as compared with the 'sobriety' of Spinoza's account of how a finite agent ought to behave. Spinoza's calm transition from 'can' to 'ought'[2] is utterly at odds with the radical exercise of freedom which takes the Kantian from 'ought' to 'can' in a single heroic act of will. However, we believe Spinoza's way ranks above its exciting rival for reasons which it is the business of this book to set forth.

---

[1] This is frequently the case with his commentators as well. For example, H. F. Hallett in his books: *Benedict de Spinoza; The Elements of his Philosophy* (The Athlone Press, London, 1957) and *Creation Emanation and Salvation: A Spinozistic Study* (Martinus Nijhoff, The Hague, 1962). The depth of Hallett's understanding is witnessed by the degree to which his own writing is found inaccessible (C. L. Hardin makes the point nicely: "It seems to me that Hallett is at the same time the most profound and the most gratuitously obscure of all the Spinoza Commentators." See 'Spinoza on Immortality and Time' in *Spinoza: New Perspectives,* ed. Robert W. Shahan, University of Oklahoma Press, Norman, 1978, note 4, p. 138.). A more accessible example is Erroll Harris in his *Spinoza: Salvation from Despair: An Appraisal of Spinoza's Philosophy* (Martinus Nijhoff, The Hague, 1973).

[2] The calm nature of this transition is captured in his notion of *acquiesentia in se ipso* (See Chapter Eight). What we ought to do is revealed to us by discovering and then accepting what we are, in fact, able to do.

Teleology is concerned with the highest good, to which it subordinates the right; consistent deontology is concerned with the right, no matter what may happen to our goods; but for the ethics of responsibility the *fitting* action, the one that fits into a total interaction as response and as anticipation of future response, is alone conducive to the good, and alone is right.

H. R. Niebuhr
The Responsible Self

CHAPTER ONE

TWO KINDS OF VALUE

Kant thought that there were two sorts of answers that can be given to the question: 'Why should I do x?' One sort is prudential and says: 'Do x because experience has shown that doing x will make you happy.' The other sort of answer is moral and says: 'Do x because x is the (morally) right thing to do.' These quite different responses point to the existence of two distinct areas in which human beings recognize value. In the first area an act may be said to have utility value if it leads to happiness. In the second area an act may be said to have moral value if it is the right thing to do under the circumstances. Thus in evaluating the utility of an act we depend entirely on the feeling the act produces in us and when this feeling is not happiness, we devalue the act. However things are very different when we are concerned with what we call moral acts. As Kant pointed out, it is the fact that the act is alleged to have been done out of respect for the rightness of the act that serves as the sole and sufficient criterion of whether such an act will have moral value: both our feelings and the consequences of the act are quite irrelevant to its moral value. In short, such acts cannot be morally devalued in the light of further experience. Their moral value is set for all time, secured through the *a priori* knowledge that to do x, y or z is morally right. Thus moral knowledge is not a species of empirical knowledge, nor is moral value a species of utility value.

These two separate areas of human value exist because we appraise our activities in two distinct ways. One way is dependent on our experience of the consequences of actions; the other way we characterize as being independent of experience, resting on a source of knowledge which is not empirical.

It was Kant who drew most sharply this line between utility value and moral value, between prudence and morality:[1]

---

[1] Cf. 'Perpetual Peace: A Philosophical Sketch' (in *CPrR*) where Kant is arguing his case that practical politics and theoretical ethics do not conflict, on the grounds that conflict does not arise—"Unless by ethics we mean a general doctrine of prudence, which would be the same as [a] theory

1

The practical law, derived from the motive of *happiness*, I term pragmatic (rule of prudence), and that law, if there is such a law, which has no other motive than *worthiness of being happy*, I term moral (law of morality). The former advises us what we have to do if we wish to achieve happiness; the latter dictates to us how we must behave in order to deserve happiness. The former is based on empirical principles; for only by means of experience can I know what desires there are which call for satisfaction; or what those natural causes are which are capable of satisfying them. The latter takes no account of desires, and the natural means of satisfying them, and considers only the freedom of a rational being in general, and the necessary conditions under which alone this freedom can harmonize with a distribution of happiness that is made in accordance with principles. This latter law can therefore be based on mere ideas of pure reason, and known *a priori*. (*CPR*, p. 636, A 806 B 834)

Kant demonstrated that the whole idea of morality (the notion that there is a way of conducting ourselves which has unconditional value[2]) only comes into being when we turn away from considerations of how happy a given way of behaving might make us and look instead to an enduring quality in our behaviour, something that stamps it with the character of being right.

He pointed out that the pursuit of happiness was an uncertain business at best[3] (there being no guarantee that past actions which have made us happy would do so in the future) whereas we could determine with

---

of the maxims for choosing the most fitting means to accomplish the purposes of self-interest. But to give this meaning to ethics is equivalent to denying that there is any such thing at all." *CPrR*, p. 331, A 67 B 72

[2] This is the essential difference between moral value and utility value. Moral value alone is good "without qualification" (*FMM*, p. 55, IV 393). In this we concur with John R. Silbur ('The moral Good and the Natural Good in Kant's Ethics', *Review of Metaphysics* 36, 1982-83, pp. 401-412): our term 'utility value' here corresponds to his term 'natural good' and has as broad a scope, i.e. it connotes happiness as a general state of well-being and not just as an immediate satisfaction.

[3] In Kant's words, "But it is a misfortune that the concept of happiness is such an indefinite concept, and that although each person wishes to attain it, he can never definitely and self-consistently state what it is he really wishes and wills. The reason for this is that all elements which belong to the concept of happiness are empirical, i.e., they must be taken from experience, while for the idea of happiness an absolute whole, a maximum, of well-being is needed in my present and in every future condition." *FMM*, p. 77, AB 46.

certainty[4] whether a given way of behaving would be morally valuable.

In the practical sphere of human action this means of determining (with certainty) that a given course of action will have moral value lies (according to Kant) in our capacity to take a given maxim[5] and universalize it. This rational procedure reveals whether the practice recommended by the maxim is self-destructive or not. The clearest example relates to the matter of lying. For instance, suppose I take as my maxim that I shall lie whenever it suits me. The procedure of attempting to universalize this maxim shows that this practice, if followed universally, would result in the destruction of the very practice which it enjoins. Thus if everyone were to lie when it suited them, no one would be able to trust anyone's word and the practice of lying would founder. When universalized, the practice of lying in order to get out of a difficult situation is seen to be practically invalid, i.e. a self-destructive practice.

This capacity to consider whether our maxims are universalizable (a capacity which is part and parcel of our capacity to reason[6]) allows us

---

[4] Our knowledge of the means to our happiness is fallible whereas we can know with certainty what to do in order to be good. Thus, given that we cannot trust reason as a reliable judge in the pursuit of happiness and that we possess reason solely in order to use it as a guide in conducting our affairs, we should—on what might well be regarded as prudential grounds—follow its lead only where it *can* guide us infallibly, viz. in the pursuit of moral value. Kant's argument to this effect is to be found in FMM, pp. 56-57, AB 4. The argument, in essence, states that since we possess Reason, an instrument ill-adapted for pursuing happiness, and if it is granted that it yet has some practical application for governing our conduct, it must be designed to serve as a means for securing the end of moral contentment, rather than happiness. We should then, from a teleological point of view, employ reason to pursue the kind of value which it is naturally suited to pursue, viz. moral value. If Kant were correct about reason, we could grant him this 'prudential' argument willingly. But we shall have cause at a later stage in the proceedings to challenge his statement that we have no infallible *instinct* for detecting that way of life which will bring us happiness. See p. 101 ff. for a fuller examination of this argument from the teleology of reason.

[5] The word 'maxim' is used in the Kantian sense: "A maxim is the subjective principle of volition. The objective principle (i.e. that which would serve all rational beings also subjectively as a practical principle if reason had full power over the faculty of desire) is the practical law." FMM, p. 62, AB 15n.

[6] This is treated in more detail on p. 59-60 below and especially in note 28 of Chapter Two.

to divide actions into those that are valid, and those that are invalid in practice. An act that is valid in practice is *permitted* from this rationally grounded (and therefore *moral*) point of view.[7] Any acts that are practically invalid are prohibited: they are said to be morally wrong.

But consider further this case of lying when circumstances call for it, lying when in difficulty. When we examine Kant's method for ruling out this practice it seems that the real source of the moral wrongness of lying rests with the uselessness of lying, with its lack of utility value as a means to the end desired. It seems that an act can only be recognized as morally wrong in virtue of the *fact* that the practice concerned can be seen, when universalized, to have unfortunate consequences. This appears to be the thrust of Kant's presentation.[8] Thus, although a given individual might well escape difficulties by lying, thereby securing happiness, if everyone followed this practice (or if any individual followed it without fail) it would prove to be self-destructive and therefore actually useless as a means of escaping from trouble. As a consequence of the procedure of universalization, a procedure which is, in effect, an imaginative projection of the effects of the proposed action, the individual *should,* Kant maintains, now see that it is morally wrong to lie *whatever* others in fact might do and whether or not they think lying will help them escape their own difficulties in the particular circumstances which face them. But it seems apparent that the force of the moral injunction is derived, not from the recognition of the unconditional wrongness of lying, but from envisaging the unfortunate consequences of universal lying, that is, from considering the imprudence of the act in question.

Kant would turn in his grave at such a supposition. He thought that he had made it abundantly clear that moral behaviour had value quite independently of the happiness which might result from it. Indeed he went so far as to argue that happiness itself could not be counted as a value unless the person who was happy *deserved*[9] to be happy by

---

[7] See *FMM*, p. 96, BA 86.

[8] cf. *FMM*, p. 81, BA 54 (second illustration).

[9] Chapter One of *FMM* opens with the famous sentence: "Nothing in the world—indeed nothing even beyond the world—can possibly be conceived which could be called good without qualification, except a *good will*." Kant continues by listing various qualities and talents that are "doubtless in many respects good and desirable" but which can also be "extremely bad and harmful if the will ... is not good." Furthermore certain desirable conditions including "the contentment with one's condition which is called happiness make for pride and even arrogance if there is not a good will to correct their influence on the mind and on its principles of

having consistently behaved according to practically valid maxims. Happiness which could not be enjoyed with a clear conscience, as we might say, was not, for Kant, real happiness at all.[10] Furthermore, happiness according to Kant was predicated upon various empirical contingencies and, although Kant acknowledged that it was something that ought to be a part of life, he maintained that it could not be pursued in a rational way as a rational goal.[11] Even with a lifetime's experience it would be impossible to learn, or reason out with certainty, what maxims to follow in order to obtain happiness. As a result, individuals who lie, thinking to thereby escape their troubles, may or may not find satisfaction in so doing. Equally the person who keeps the moral law in order to escape a greater trouble that might arise if they lied would be in a similar predicament. Such a person who obeys the moral law for prudential reasons could not be sure of success in obtaining happiness. Kant is saying then that, if happiness is set up as the one value worth actualizing, there is no certain procedure to follow in order to achieve it.

Thus although the Categorical Imperative[12] might seem ultimately to derive its capacity as a detector of *moral* maxims through reference to *prudential* considerations, in fact its force is not so based, because following moral maxims as an exercise in prudence does not guarantee happiness as an outcome.

Kant needs to emphasize the fact that moral value can be secured simply by obeying the moral law *for its own sake*—regardless of the consequences in terms of utility value. However there is a problem associated with this independent characterization of moral value. Granted that the process whereby moral value is created is open to us, i.e. that we *can* do our duty for duty's sake, why would anyone want to realize this

---

action, so as to make it universally conformable to its end." As a consequence of this, and of the belief that there is something irrational and unfair about Fortune being kind to those of ill-will, Kant concludes that "the good will seems to constitute the indispensable condition even of worthiness to be happy." *FMM*, p. 55, BA 1-2.

[10] Cf. John R. Silber, 'The Importance of the Highest Good in Kant's Ethics', *Ethics* 73 1962- 1963.

[11] See Note 4 to Chapter One.

[12] Leaving aside the debates on the various formulations of the Categorical Imperative—the moral law—we focus on the *CPrR* formulation which describes the process of universalizing thus: [the] "Fundamental Law of Pure Practical Reason [is]: So act that the maxim of your will could always hold at the same time as the principle of a universal legislation." *CPrR*, p. 142, A 54.

kind of value in their lives? Is it, for example, satisfying or enjoyable to behave morally?

Kant's answer to this question is deeply paradoxical. Yes, he says, moral behaviour is satisfying. The consciousness of having acted solely out of duty is characterized by a feeling of self-contentment which is analogous to happiness.[13] Indeed this feeling of self-contentment is superior in value to happiness in that happiness can lose its value—its satisfying character—if it is the consequence of immoral behaviour. Self-contentment, by contrast, is a species of satisfaction which has unconditional value. However this satisfaction which self-contentment brings has a curious feature: it can only be obtained if it is not sought as the end of moral behaviour. Indeed, it is a function of indifference to ends. If you are motivated by a desire for self-contentment, then it will not be self-contentment that you feel as a result of your action. Moral behaviour is an end in itself and must be practised for its own sake. As soon as the maxim of one's action includes the aim of feeling self-contentment, the maxim ceases to be pure and the behaviour it gives rise to can no longer be called moral. The unique nature of this moral feeling of self-contentment (a satisfying feeling that is achieved through moral behaviour, but which amounts to a state of satisfaction which cannot itself be the point of behaving morally) constitutes the paradoxical aspect of Kant's answer to our question. When asked, 'Is it really worthwhile behaving morally?', Kant is unable to respond in a simple yes/no fashion. On the one hand it is worthwhile in that self-contentment is definitely worth experiencing.[14] However this is not where the worth, the value, of moral action lies. It lies rather in being determined to act by reason alone.[15] You can only act morally if you are, in fact, unconcerned with what is to be gained from your action. Moral value can be brought into being only if you recognize that self-contentment, happiness, or anything other than the moral law itself, is beside the point when the moral value of one's present behaviour is assessed. In short, moral

---

[13] In Kant's "Critical Resolution of the Antinomy of Practical Reason" we read: "Thus we can understand how the consciousness of this capacity of a pure practical reason through a deed (virtue) can produce a consciousness of mastery over inclinations and thus of independence from them and from the discontentment which always accompanies them, bringing forth a negative satisfaction with one's condition, i.e., contentment, whose source is contentment with one's own person." *CPrR*, p. 222, A 213

[14] cf. *CPrR*, p. 222, A 213: "Freedom itself thus becomes in this indirect way capable of an enjoyment."

[15] See *CPrR*, p. 220, A 210.

behaviour is good in itself. Its goodness does not lie in any state of consciousness which it brings about—even though it does, as a matter of fact, produce a satisfying state of consciousness, viz. a feeling of self-contentment.

The Antinomy of Practical Reason

From what has been said about self-contentment it would appear that virtue (moral behaviour) is always rewarded by this analogue of happiness. It would also seem that although self-contentment must not be sought as an end, it will—willy-nilly—provide virtuous persons with a source of satisfaction which will be sufficient to compensate for whatever lack of contingent happiness falls to their lot, especially if this unhappiness comes as a direct result of their doing their duty according to the moral law. And this might seem to be the end of the matter: as long as we accept the paradoxical nature of self-contentment as a reward that can only come if it is not sought,[16] then we see that, though self-contentment cannot be the source of moral value, it serves to compensate moral agents for their willingness to forego their natural desire for happiness. The situation is a bit baroque, but the accounts balance.

However, Kant is not satisfied with having self-contentment as a straight substitute for happiness. He specifically designates it as a 'negative satisfaction' and distinguishes it from happiness proper, which involves "a positive participation of feeling."[17] In the Analytic of the *CPrR* he argues

> That virtue (as the worthiness to be happy) is the supreme condition of whatever appears to us to be desirable and thus of all our pursuit of happiness and, consequently, that it is the supreme good... (*CPrR*, p. 215, A 198)

He continues

> But these truths do not imply that [virtue] is the entire and perfect good as the object of the faculty of desire of rational finite beings. In order to be this, happiness is also required... For to be in need of happiness and also worthy of it and yet not to partake of it could not be in accordance

---

[16] This does, in fact, accord with our experience of the disinterested kind of satisfaction that follows when we do something for its own sake, or simply just do it well.

[17] *CPrR*, p. 222, A 214.

with the complete volition of an omnipotent rational being, if we assume such only for the sake of the argument. (*CPrR*, p. 215, A 198-199)

Kant here recognizes that, for human beings, an ideal state includes *both* virtue *and* happiness, i.e. the highest good.[18] However to characterize human beings as creatures which are motivated by such a composite desire raises a dilemma. As rational, a human being is required—in virtue of its rationality—to pursue virtue alone, but the *finite* rational being we are concerned with, viz. the human being, also desires those positive participations of feeling that Kant recognizes as constitutive of human happiness. Reason provides clear-cut rules for pursuing virtue, but is unable to provide any certain rules for pursuing happiness. Any finite rational being is thus faced with a personal

---

[18] cf. *CPrR*, p. 199, A 166: "But this distinction of the principle of happiness from that of morality is not for this reason an *opposition* between them, and pure practical reason does not require that we should renounce the claims to happiness; it requires *only that we take no account of them whenever duty is in question.*"

Much debate has been entered into concerning the success or otherwise of Kant's maintaining this distinction without opposition by way of the concept of the highest good. See for example:

John R. Silber. 'Kant's Conception of the Highest Good as Immanent and Transcendent' *Philosophical Review* **68** 1959

John R. Silber. 'The Importance of the Highest Good in Kant's Ethics' *Ethics* **73** 1962-1963

John R. Silber. 'Der Schematismus der Praktischen Vernunft' *Kant-Studien* **56** 1965

John R. Silber. 'The Moral Good and the Natural Good in Kant's Ethics' *Review of Metaphysics* **36** 1982-1983

L.W. Beck, *A Commentary on Kant's Critique of Practical Reason*, University of Chicago Press, Chicago, 1960, Chapter XIII

Jeffrie G. Murphy, 'The Highest Good as Content for Kant's Ethical Formalism' *Kant-Studien* **56** 1965-1966

Mary-Barbara Zelden, 'The Summum Bonum, The Moral Law and the Existence of God' *Kant-Studien* **62** 1971-1972

Klaus Dusing, 'Das Problem des Hochsten Gutes in Kants Praktische Philosophie' *Kant-Studien* **62** 1971-1972

John Beversluis, 'Kant on Moral Striving' *Kant-Studien* **62** 1971-1972

Thomas Auxter, 'The Unimportance of Kant's Highest Good', *The Journal of the History of Philosophy* **27** 1979

We are indebted to these articles as a fruitful ground for working out our understanding of the respective roles of virtue and happiness in Kant's philosophy and of the relationship which he endeavours to establish between them.

dilemma. Such a being wants happiness but has no absolutely reliable guide for attaining it. Such beings also want virtue but they can only attain it if they cast aside their desire for happiness. It seems then that although human beings have, as their natural end, the highest good—a combination of virtue and happiness—they cannot seek it, since they cannot seek both to be virtuous and to be happy in one and the same act.

...the maxims of virtue and those of one's own happiness are wholly heterogeneous and ... they strongly limit and check each other in the same subject. (*CPrR*, p. 217, A 202-203)

The very existence of this conception of the highest good appears therefore to involve an Antinomy.[19] Reason acknowledges the concept of the highest good, the notion of a necessary connection between virtue and happiness, to be "an *a priori* necessary object of our will"[20] while at the same time ruling out the possibility of rationally pursuing this goal since a rational will can only pursue virtue when it ceases to pursue happiness (and *vice versa*).

So far as Kant is concerned there is no way to avoid this antinomy, no reformulation of the problem[21] which would eliminate its basic cause—the existence of two radically different types of value. Kant's conviction that there are these two types of value—moral and prudential—is just one expression of a deeper conviction that lies at the very foundation of his philosophy, viz. the heterogeneity of sense and reason in human nature. A human being, for Kant,[22] is an animal rational,[23] a combination of

---

[19] An antinomy is a form of transcendental illusion arising when Reason produces contradictory positions yet can give up neither. In the Antinomy of Practical Reaon, Reason demonstrates that, although both virtue and happiness are necessary ingredients in the highest good (our natural goal) they cannot both be pursued at once.

[20] *CPrR*, p. 218, A 205.

[21] With reference to the discussion of the correct formulation of an Antinomy involving the concept of the highest good in Book's *A Commentary on Kant's Critique of Practical Reason* (University of Chicago Press, Chicago, 1960) it is not our intention here to ignore Beck's argument concerning the weakness of Kant's formulation of the Antinomy, nor to overlook Beck's proposed reformulation. Beck's presentation of the opposition (between virtue and happiness) involved in the concept of the highest good is undoubtedly more logically sound than Kant's. Our contention is simply that, whatever the formulation, the opposition between virtue and happiness cannot be explained away.

[22] See *CJ*, CaJ p. 73, A 49 B 50.

[23] This is to be contrasted with Aristotle's view of man as a rational

two separate natures, the sensible and the rational. Animals are commonly thought to have entirely sensible natures. And it is possible to conceive of beings that are entirely rational—Kant's intelligible Author of Nature being a prime example.[24] However in human beings, these two natures appear together.[25] The heterogeneity of sense and reason means that human nature is a unique mixture. Neither sense nor reason is naturally subordinated to the other: sense is not plastic to the demands of reason and reason is not the slave of sense.

We have seen that this being who possesses a mixed nature recognizes value in two areas of its experience: a naturally occurring (and in that sense, basic) value, expressed in terms of the happiness that follows upon engaging in certain lines of action as these are prompted by desires, and a moral value which can be achieved through the act of willing in accordance with what is known, *a priori*, to be the right thing to do. Now happiness is the object of desire for a human being in so far as its nature is sensible. This basic value therefore belongs to the area of human experience that is a function of our sensible nature, i.e. our happiness-seeking nature. Moral value belongs to that area of our activities that is solely a function of our rational nature and Kant makes it quite clear that happiness and moral value cannot be assimilated one to the other:

happiness and morality are two specifically different elements of the highest good and therefore their combination cannot be known analytically (as if a person who sought his happiness found himself virtuous merely through solving his problem, or one who followed virtue found himself *ipso facto* happy in the consciousness of this conduct). (*CPrR*, p. 217, A 203)

Now it is worth noting in this context that Kant has no difficulty in disposing of the first of these alternatives: it is, he maintains[26], "absolutely false ... [to hold that] striving for happiness produces a

---

animal. For Aristotle, man is the rational species of the the genus 'animal'. But it seems that for Kant, man is the animal species of the genus 'Rational Being'. Stanley Cavell makes the point nicely in *The Claim of Reason*, Clarendon Press, Oxford, 1979, p. 399.

[24] See *CPrR*, p. 219, A 207.
[25] See e.g. MM, pp. 80-83, A 65-69. cf. *CJ*, CtJ p. 99, A 393-394 B 398-399 and *CPR*, p. 465, A 534 B 562.
[26] *CPrR*, p. 218, A 206.

ground for the virtuous disposition." If we are to be moral (on Kant's understanding of morality[27]) we must indeed *shun* the pursuit of happiness. However the second alternative (that a virtuous disposition *ipso facto* produces happiness) gives Kant pause. He finds it strange that many philosophers, particularly among the Ancients, have failed to recognize the contingency of the connection between happiness and virtue "in *this* life."[28] So far as he can see, experience shows us quite plainly that happiness is rarely meted out in just proportion to virtue.[29] Kant proceeds to explain this curious fact (that, on the face of it, he seems to be out of step with the majority of thinkers on this particular subject) by pointing out that the happiness these philosophers refer to is not, strictly speaking, happiness at all. That is to say, it is not the kind of happiness that is the object of sensible desire. Although these philosophers prized it as such, what they were really talking about was self-contentment, a term which "in its real meaning refers only to [a] negative satisfaction..."[30] It is not the result of the satisfaction of any inclination, not even of an inclination to do one's duty. Self-contentment results only when one's sensuous nature is not in the ascendant, when the positive satisfaction we call happiness is not the concern. Self-contentment, says Kant, "cannot be called happiness, since it does not depend upon a positive participation of feeling."[31] The belief that happiness does accord with virtue in this life is therefore simply a function of incorrect usage of the terms involved. The experience that accompanies virtue is not a feeling of happiness: it is a feeling of self-contentment.

In these efforts to correct usage, Kant seeks to show that there cannot be any empirical warrant for the view that following the virtuous course of action is an actual cause of happiness. Apparent evidence that people can find themselves *ipso facto* happy in the consciousness of their virtue is to be explained away by appeals to how correct usage would characterize these apparent instances of happiness. Although people may feel happy when they have been virtuous and be quite certain that it is

---

[27] See note 1 to Chapter One.

[28] *CPrR*, p. 219, A 208.

[29] cf. *CJ*, CtJ p. 121, A 422, B427: "He may, it is true expect to find a chance concurrence now and again, but he can never expect to find in nature a uniform agreement—a consistent agreement according to fixed rules, answering to what his maxims are and must be subjectively, with that end [the highest good] which yet he feels himself obliged and urged to realize."

[30] *CPrR*, p. 221, A 212.

[31] *ibid.*, p. 222, A 214.

happiness they feel (a positive feeling similar to what they feel when their desires are satisfied) Kant would still say that such people had made a mistake: they have misinterpreted their experience.

"Something is Rotten in the State of Denmark"

In the light of this 'correction' (which, as we shall see,[32] is only one of a number of such reinterpretations of common experience which Kant makes in the course of his defence of morality as a legitimate form of life) the question must arise as to why he was so confident about making it. In our view he simply has to make this adjustment, given his background theory of human nature. As we shall see, Kant is wedded to a theory which requires these corrections, a theory which, under pressure from recalcitrant empirical evidence, forces its author to cast about for some way of reinterpreting the evidence so that it will fall in line with the demands of the theory. Kant must therefore face the accusation that his theory is adjusting the facts rather than adjusting to them. *Prima facie*, this accusation is supported by ordinary usage which treats self-contentment as a positive feeling. It is something people long for and which they follow the path of virtue to secure. The possession of this feeling seems a clear instance of being happy and as a consequence, virtue can be classified as something which has utility value for those who would be happy.

Now despite this *prima facie* evidence against his view, Kant insisted that the value of virtuous behaviour is not dependent on any feelings of happiness which might occur as a consequence. To fly thus in the face of common experience[33] Kant must have been convinced that his theory regarding the independence of moral value was necessarily true, that it was true *a priori*. For we can fairly presume that only an *a priori* conviction would have had the power to force him to reinterpret aspects of our experience in such a way as to contradict widely-held beliefs.

Moreover, Kant's conviction that morality could be given an *a priori* foundation had a basis in experience. The unconditional value of moral

---

[32] There are several such reinterpretations. For a full examination of these see Chapter Seven.

[33] It may be argued that common experience verifies Kant's views on the nature of the moral feeling of self-contentment, viz, his view that it is a feeling of independence from desire which is not a variety of happiness. But this is an interpretation of our experience that can be challenged and indeed this challenge is a central aspect of what we have to say in this book. See Chapter Seven, below.

behaviour (virtue as the supreme good) was, so far as he could see, a robust phenomenon.[34] He felt it was quite evident that people value moral behaviour above happiness, that they see absolute goodness residing only in the moral sphere and regard the 'goods' conducive to happiness as being only relative and conditional.[35] Yet despite the existence of these beliefs (which indicate a popular appreciation of the distinction between moral value and utility value), Kant recognized that there was a real problem with regard to the reality of moral value in the following sense: people could always doubt in a given instance whether a given act was morally valuable or whether it had in fact been motivated by ulterior considerations.[36] The very existence of this doubt (the doubt about ulterior motives) raises a fundamental objection to morality as a form of life: perhaps we are not, in fact, capable of acting *solely* out of the thought of duty. Perhaps ulterior motives are always present. How, after all, could we act unless we were somehow motivated to do so? Kant is convinced that we can act solely out of duty, but how is he to explain the possibility of so acting?

Now so far as Kant was concerned no behaviour (as a natural event) can arise without a cause: the empirical model of human behaviour was understood by him to be deterministic. Furthermore, the cause of a given piece of behaviour had to be a naturally arising desire for some satisfaction.[37] Against this background the mere possibility of a moral act, an act which is not premised on a desire for satisfaction (happiness) demands an explanation. Kant's question: 'How can reason be practical?' (or 'How can a person act solely from duty?'[38]) must, he felt, be answerable, for if it is not, then the demands of reason (as presented in the moral law and our sense of duty) will be vain and empty.[39] However, Kant insisted that our consciousness of the moral law, our

---

[34] cf. *CPrR*, p. 214-215, A 198: "that unconditioned condition, i.e., the condition which is subordinate to no other..." And further: "That virtue (as the worthiness to be happy) is the supreme condition of whatever appears to us to be desirable and thus of all our pursuit of happiness and consequently that it is the supreme good have been proven in the Analytic."

[35] See the opening passage of *FMM*, p. 55, BA 1.

[36] The problem of subreption see pp. 54 *ff.*, below.

[37] "Life is the faculty of a being by which it acts according to the laws of the faculty of desire. The *faculty of desire* is the faculty such a being has of causing, through its ideas, the reality of the objects of these ideas." *CPR*, p. 124 n., A 16 n.

[38] See *CPrR*, p. 129, A 30-31.

[39] See *CPrR*, p. 218, A 205.

awareness of the moral force of the term 'ought', provides a *prima facie* indication that we have the ability to do what the law prescribes. In other words, Kant was convinced that the very existence of morality as an acknowledged form of life was grounds for the presumption that 'ought' implies 'can'.[40] If we could not do what Reason orders us to do, then the idea of Reason having the authority to command us (an idea which is at the heart of the moral form of life) would be unintelligible.

So, given that people do feel the moral force of 'ought', it must be the case that they *can* act on reason's dictates (which embody the moral law). (If they could not, the whole idea of their feeling *obliged* to act as the moral law prescribes, would be unintelligible.) However, if they can so act, then there must be some explanation of how this is possible and since a natural causal factor, e.g. a desire for happiness, cannot be responsible for moral behaviour, there must be some analogous 'causal' factor which can explain how this behaviour is possible.

A Shadow Model of Moral Causality

The explanation of how things happen in terms of natural causality involves the use of a certain interrelated set of concepts, what Wittgenstein called a 'language-game'. The explanation, for example, of the process whereby human beings pursue and achieve happiness is couched in terms of the following:

a) a naturally occurring cause or motive, viz. a desire for a specific satisfaction. This is associated with

b) an effect: the performance of an action which is recognized to be the means to the desired end. This, when it is successful, produces

c) a satisfaction: an experience of happiness which marks the fulfilment of the desire which initiated the process.

When, however, we speak of moral behaviour, the character of the

---

[40] Awareness of the moral law is the *ratio cognoscendi* of freedom (See *CPrR*, p. 119 n., A 5 n.): It grounds the ability to act morally. The moral law is our ground for knowing that we are free and for knowing the extent of our abilities. This does not mean that *any* feeling of obligation that any person may feel necessarily entails their ability to fulfill it. Rather (following John R. Silber,'Kant's Conception of the Highest Good as Immanent and Transcendent' *Philosopohical Review* 68 1959, pp. 47ff) the overall feeling of moral duty presupposes a rudimentary ability to act in accordance with duty independently of feelings ('ought' presupposes 'can') i.e. it *informs* us of this. We can thus, in Kant's view, infer from this general sense of 'ought' to a freedom to act.

explanation which sets out how it is to be actualized must, of necessity, be different. As Kant has emphasized, the actualization of moral value has nothing to do with the satisfaction of desire. And yet, if this explanation is to *sound* like an explanation, something like the natural causality language-game must be employed since this is the vehicle through which the concept of something being explained gets its meaning. As we shall see, an analogue of the natural causality language-game—in effect, a *shadow* language-game—comes into play when the phenomenon to be explained is moral behaviour.

Our decision to call this analogue of natural causality a 'shadow' of it is a function of the fact that the only model of causality we have is also our sole model of what an explanation should be like. In order for Kant's answer to the question 'How can reason be practical?' to present itself as an explanation, it must reproduce, term for term, the concepts employed in the natural causality language-game which provides the structure of what we ordinarily call an explanation. Such a model is, therefore, not unfairly called a 'shadow' in that it follows in outline the form of the original. However, to say that it is a shadow of the original is not to imply that it is insubstantial, that it does not really explain anything or that it cannot be understood as so doing. In fact, as we shall see, we cannot insult the shadow model of causality by exposing its failure to explain how moral behaviour is possible, for this, in a perverse way, is its virtue.

When Kant introduced a shadow model of causality in order to answer the question of how reason can be practical, he was very much aware that this shadow model—so long as it is judged by the model of explanation constituted by natural causality—was not a success. It is never able to explain, but only to 'explain' the possibility of moral behaviour.[41] And indeed the very failure of his 'explanation' served as a sort of 'reverse' *reductio ad absurdum* argument for the completely unique character of moral value and the behaviour which actualizes it. Thus if his shadow explanation *did* explain how reason could be practical, then it would have failed in virtue of the fact that it would have exposed moral behaviour as natural (which is to say, explicable), thereby assimilating moral behaviour to natural behaviour. Explaining morality in this sense necessarily explains it away since, by definition, it cannot be explained according to natural causality. Natural causality (insofar as it concerns

---

[41] See *CPrR*, p. 180, A 128: "For how a law in itself can be the direct determining ground of the will (which is the essence of morality) is an insoluble problem for the human reason."

itself with human behaviour) involves, as its engine, the desire for happiness and nothing driven by this engine can constitute moral behaviour. So we cannot attack Kant's 'explanation' of moral behaviour simply on the grounds that it is not a *natural* explanation.[42]

However, Kant's answer to the question of how reason can be practical does have an Achilles' heel. In the course of expounding his shadow explanation Kant makes use of various empirical phenomena which describe the inner life of a person engaged in moral behaviour. A person concerned with acting morally experiences feelings peculiar to such a concern, feelings which have a distinctively moral flavour: a sense of duty or obligation; a feeling of awe for the rightness of what is right; a feeling of respect that acting in accordance with this rightness generates; a sense of dignity which arises when a person acknowledges the primacy of the moral law and acts accordingly; and, finally, a feeling of self-contentment experienced when one has succeeded in willing according to maxims which are morally right. These phenomena play a considerable role in Kant's description of the shadow model of moral causality and serve as evidence to persuade his readers that the moral form of life is plausible. They present morality as a complex form of life made up of elements familiar to us from our experience of our own inner lives.

However, since this evidence is empirical, it is open to an explanation in terms of natural causality. If the 'moral flavour' of these phenomena can be dissipated, if we can show that the 'moral' elements of our inner life can be explained without reference to the moral form of life which Kant champions, then the plausibility of Kant's 'explanation' of how reason can be practical will be undermined.

We believe that Spinoza's understanding of human behaviour can provide the model for a natural explanation of the various phenomena which Kant cited in his attempts to defend the plausibility of moral behaviour. However, as we shall see, Spinoza's explanation is natural in a special sense of this word:[43] it entails no mere reductive dissolution of moral values to natural values. It will therefore be argued that it is capable of doing justice to and does not merely explain away, the special quality of moral behaviour which Kant had seized upon as evidence that there was an aspect of human behaviour which was not explicable as the outcome of natural (empirical) causes.

Our initial step in this enterprise will be to set out Kant's shadow model of moral causality in some detail.

---

[42] cf. e.g. *FMM*, pp. 100-101, BA 94.

[43] We will be using the term 'agent-naturalism' to mark this special sense.

CHAPTER TWO

KANT'S SHADOW MODEL OF MORAL CAUSALITY

The question that concerns Kant in his second Critique is this: how can reason be practical? This might look like a question about the role that reasoning plays in action and the straightforward answer to this question, outside the Kantian context, would be an explanation of the place reasoning has in human action set out in terms of natural causality. Natural causality, as Kant understood it, is a sequence of events in which an earlier event (the cause) is connected to a succeeding event (the effect) according to a rule.[1] Thus when we wish to explain human behaviour in terms of natural causality this will involve a description of several events including the agent's reasoning. Typically this description makes reference to a given stimulus arousing a desire for something which in turn sets in motion the process of working out, through reasoning (based on the given information and past experience), the best means to the end in view. This in turn leads directly to appropriate action and to satisfaction as the motivating desire is fulfilled.

When there is more than one desire the situation, although more complicated, can still be expressed in terms of a single unbroken causal sequence. In this case, two separate stimuli lead to the more or less simultaneous activation of two distinct desires. Subsequent experience reveals the fact that both desires cannot be achieved at once and one or the other must be given precedence. There follows a felicific calculation[2] in which the strongest desire makes itself known. In effect this calculation amounts to a weighing-up of the pros and cons of satisfying one or other

---

[1] See *CPR*, p. 464, A 532 B 560. "When we are dealing with what happens there are only two kinds of causality conceivable by us; the causality is either according to *nature* or arises from *freedom*. The former is the connection in the sensible world of one state with a preceding state on which it follows according to a rule."

[2] The terminology is Bentham's but here it is being used to refer to the fact that left to ourselves, we, like all animals, are able to come up with (as if automatically calculated) the answer to the question: 'What will please me most?' (or 'Which course of action do I prefer?').

of the competing desires, a process accomplished (so far as the agent is concerned) by simply considering which course of action, on balance, will produce the greatest satisfaction. When this becomes apparent, action follows and the agent achieves satisfaction.

As with any natural explanation, there are no gaps in the causal sequence. Each step in the sequence is naturally determined ('brought about') by the prior steps. Thus there is no place for any free exercise of the will as an intervening factor as we might suppose when, for example, we think of ourselves as choosing between competing desires. Where we are employing a natural explanation schema, the *decision* to pursue one course of action rather than the other is not to be understood as a distinct element intervening and so governing the course of the causal sequence. Instead the decision must be regarded as a function of the relative strengths of the desires in question as these emerge in the consideration of the likely consequences of pursuing alternative courses of action. We call the discovery, through felicific calculation, of the strongest desire a *decision* only in retrospect in order to call attention to the point at which we became aware that one of our desires outweighed the other. To sum up: as a component in the natural causal sequence which is initiated by those stimuli which prompt desires in us, reasoning does not determine (in the sense of choose) which desire will be supreme.

This natural model of explanation for human behaviour we will dub the original model. We now wish to show how the shadow model of moral behaviour is developed from the original and to see how the shadow model deviates from the original as a kind of explanation.

Kant's question in the *Critique of Practical Reason* ('How can reason be Practical?') concerns the possibility of reason functioning so as to direct human behaviour by itself, as it were, and not simply as the servant of desire. For it is Kant's view that reason is not limited to an advisory role, the role it plays in formulating hypothetical imperatives: 'If you want x (some satisfaction) then it would be rational to do y.' This Kant refers to as the heteronomous function of reason. But in its most important function, Kant was convinced that reason is to be regarded as *autonomous*, supplying its own motivation and its own satisfaction and thus not serving as a mere tool of external motivations supplied by the faculty of desire.[3]

Now Kant is convinced that reason *must* be practical since, if it were not, morality would be impossible and moral ideals empty. But since, in his view, morality manifestly exists as a form of

---

[3] See *CPrR*, pp. 144-145, A 58-59 Theorem IV.

life,[4] he concentrates on providing an explanation of how such autonomous rational behaviour is brought about rather than whether it ever actually occurs. That is, Kant concentrates on supplying a model which will serve to explain reason's practical capacity to produce moral behaviour. This system of moral causality (what we have called the 'shadow model of causality') is needed because the mechanism of natural causality is inappropriate to explain moral behaviour. It is inappropriate because it has no place for reasoning as an autonomous practical faculty. As we have seen, the original model describes rational human behaviour as determined naturally, i.e. as activated or set into operation by a heteronomous influence, viz. desire. Any explanation of human behaviour on this natural model (the original) leaves no room for the imputation of responsibility to the person who acts, since everything a person does is understood as a direct consequence of some naturally occurring desire. There is simply no room then in this model for an autonomous, a self-governing, principle of action. But this is precisely what is required if the action in question is to be thought of as lying within the agent's responsibility. However, an explanation of moral behaviour—if it is to sound like an *explanation*—must describe a linked series of events that are related as cause to effect and which, altogether, account for how the behaviour that is to be explained has come about. The explanation of moral behaviour must therefore be at least analogous to explanations of behaviour in terms of natural causality. To repeat: the model of moral behaviour must be modelled on the original model of non-moral behaviour if it is to present itself *as* an explanation.

What then does the shadow model which explains moral causality (i.e. *how* reason can be practical) amount to? Moral behaviour as a form of life arises from a new kind of internal conflict. As we have seen, when we experience conflicting natural desires, a resolution of this conflict is effected through reason's investigations which allow us to calculate (felicifically) which desire is likely (when we carefully consider the consequences which reason lays before us) to bring the greatest satisfaction. However, in the case of morality, the internal conflict which marks the appearance of morality as a form of life is a conflict between a

---

[4] *ibid.*, p. 143, A 56 and p. 157, A 81, where the moral law is considered to be a "fact of pure reason." See also p. 152, A 72, in which the argument of the Analytic is summed up: the fact of autonomy in the principle of morality proves that pure reason can be practical. Kant is thoroughly convinced that we would not have the idea of the moral law, especially as a *compelling* directive, if it were not possible to effect its unconditional demands. Cf. note 42 to Chapter One.

natural desire to do something and a sense of duty which is felt as a constraint upon this natural desire. In the shadow model of moral causality, this sense of duty or feeling of obligation plays the role that desire plays in the original model. The sense of duty or obligation constitutes a new sort of 'desire', a 'desire' to do what is right. But as an element within the shadow model of moral causality it cannot have any actual motivational power as desires do. If it did, then moral behaviour would result only when our feelings of obligation were, *as a matter of fact*, stronger than the natural desire that they set themselves against. In such a case, we would not be acting freely, out of a sense of duty, but simply *because* of the strength of our feelings of obligation. In other words, the moral behaviour of the agent would have a natural explanation, and thus have no *moral* value.

The sequence of events which constitutes the moral form of life and at the same time illustrates the shadow model of moral causality can be usefully set out through the form of a dialogue for reasons which become apparent as the dialogue progresses and which will be dealt with explicitly later.[5]

With any piece of behaviour, natural or moral, the action is instigated by some stimulus. In the example to be presented it is the arrival of an account in the post.

Desire: I am inclined to pay this account for the usual reason: failure to pay will result in the repossession of the item in question which is a source of satisfaction to me. I am therefore inclined to pay because I want to continue to enjoy the item.

Reason: I can appreciate that, but we lack the funds to pay this bill. I suggest we either give up x or borrow the money we need.

Desire: Let's borrow the money.

Reason: But you[6] cannot repay it. You will have to lie to convince the lender to give you the money.

Desire: Who cares? I want satisfaction.

At this point the natural sequence (following the original model of natural causality) would continue along the usual lines:

Reason: I can appreciate that, but would it be wise to blindly pursue

---

[5] See pp. 35 *ff.*, below, especially p. 39.

[6] There is a certain amount of confusion as to who is the 'person' in charge here. This confusion reflects an unavoidable problem when the faculties are personified. See pp. 39 *ff.* below where this problem is discussed.

this satisfaction? What happens when the lender is not paid?

Desire: Borrow again.

Reason: Word will get around, and no one will lend you money in the future (it's happened to others).

Desire: I wouldn't like that.[7]

Reason: No. Best perhaps to give up x now and retain your reputation, since it might come in handy later. If you follow your inclination you will eventually lose both x and your reputation.

Desire: I guess I'll take your advice.

Here the felicific calculus is at work weighing the thought of a present (short-term) pleasure against considerations relating to long-term pleasures and pains. The balance could tip either way depending on past experience which supplies the felicific 'weights' which are thrown into the balance when such thoughts occupy our attention.

Let us now consider the moral resolution of this conflict. (The moral sequence follows on Desire's remark: "Who cares? I want satisfaction.")

Conscience: I can appreciate that, but would it be right[8] to borrow money knowing that you cannot repay it, that is, lie to get what you want?[9]

Conscience then asks Reason a strange question.

What would things be like if everyone adopted the maxim for action that Desire wants to act upon?

Reason: The practice of lying would necessarily self-destruct if universally practised. It is a practically invalid maxim.

Here we must break into the dialogue to ask: "Who is this Conscience character?" Whence comes this voice of Conscience which asks its reproachful question: 'Would it be right?' Within the original model Reason can ask a rather similar question on the basis of past experience, viz. 'Would it be wise?' and proceed to adumbrate prudential

---

[7] This is a crucial step in the 'natural' procedure. If Desire does not react emotionally to Reason's imaginative projection, then Reason's argument will have no power.

[8] This question marks the appearance of the phenomenon of a sense of duty, unique to the 'inner life' of a person behaving morally. See p. 16, above.

[9] Notice how suddenly Conscience makes its entrance. This is also the case in the Kantian original. See *FMM*, p. 81, BA 54.

considerations. However, Conscience does not speak with the voice of experience, but from another quarter altogether. Conscience is, it would seem, the *categorical* voice of Reason:[10] in Kant's terminology, the pure as opposed to the empirical aspect of practical reason.[11] Here we have Reason speaking not as the hypothesizing guide to happiness, computing the best means to achieve satisfaction on the basis of past experience, but rather speaking on its own behalf of a completely different goal—a goal which has nothing to do with happiness. Thus the first assumption of the shadow model of moral causality is that we are capable of being motivated by this goal, that we can 'desire' it even though we do not desire it in the natural sense of desiring, e.g. desiring food when we are hungry. Can we make any sense out of this notion of being motivated to do what is right?

We can provide an answer to this question by asking what interest Conscience (the categorical voice of Reason) might have in our doing what is right? Why does it want us to do what is right? It speaks as if it mattered to it what we did, as if it cared. It *reproaches* us with its question: 'But would it be right?' The tone of its question indicates clearly that it feels we ought to do what is right and in some sense of the word it *wants* us to heed its reproach. One way of appreciating its motivation here is to say that it wants us to do what it would do if it were able to act.

We can begin to appreciate why Conscience exhibits this attitude by considering what constitutes the character of this action that it wants us to perform and that it labels 'right'. The hallmark of reasoning is consistency and, *were Reason (for whom Conscience speaks) a person, an agent,* we can suppose that it would always *act* according to maxims which were consistent, i.e. practically valid. In other words, it would always act on maxims which did not self-destruct when put into practice. But if we ask: 'Why would it so act?', 'What would motivate it?', we

---

[10] Notice how 'Reason' rather than 'reason' seems appropriate here. This is also the practice followed in the various translations of Kant's works in which we find 'Reason', 'Sensibility', 'Understanding' and 'Judgment', all capitalized. The process of personification which, as we shall see later, the dialogue form entails, shifts attention from active functions of, for example, reasoning, to something which performs this function—Reason. The fact that we identify with this 'something' (for it is we who are reasoning, i.e. the something is a someone, a person), has us naturally treating reason as a person and is thus deserving of a proper name.

[11] As in the question at the centre of *CPrR*: "Is pure reason sufficient of itself to determine the will, or is it only as empirically conditioned that it can do so?" *CPrR*, p. 129, A 30.

must grant that it would not do so through desire, since reason, even personified, is not burdened with desires. It follows, if we allow some substance to this personification,[12] that it can only have one other sort of motivation which, in some fashion at least, is intelligible to us: if Reason were a person it would always act consistently *simply in order to be what it is*. Just as we might insist that invalid reasoning is not reasoning insofar as we cannot 'follow' invalid arguments, so, by analogy, practically invalid acting could not be construed as Reason acting, since such acts self-destruct: they are not rational acts. So the 'interest' that Reason (as personified and speaking with the voice of Conscience) has in getting us to obey its injunctions can be thought of as being ontologically based.[13] The trope of personification, which a description of the moral form of life quite naturally falls into, leads to the somewhat curious conclusion that Conscience wants us to do our duty, wants us to *be* good, so that it can be (behave) in accordance with its own nature, and thus be true to itself (a goal which is characteristic of the moral form of life). Thus a key element of the shadow model of moral causality is the occurence within us of a sense of duty which is felt as a kind of imposition. We feel it as an admonition presented by one of our faculties to behave as it would if it could, viz. in accordance with maxims which are practically valid.

Now, in reality, Reason cannot act without our being willing to actualize its commands in our lives. Therefore, proving that Reason *can be* practical involves showing "that freedom does in fact belong to the human will":[14] in other words showing that we can will to be reasonable (to do what is right) without reference to natural motives. We understand, then, that Reason, as personified, is only an abstraction. It must not, therefore, be regarded as capable of actually coercing us into doing its bidding by awakening within us a feeling of obligation which then determines us to act after the fashion of a natural motive. If morality is to be possible Reason's categorical *persona*, Conscience, can, it seems, only 'coerce' us by setting up a standard of practically valid behaviour which it would pursue if it could act (viz. dutiful behaviour) and then leaving us the choice[15] as to whether its 'desires' are to be

---

[12] Such an allowance is necessary once the trope of personification is employed and, as we shall see below (pp. 42 *ff.*), its use is a natural result of a certain aspect of reflexive consciousness which will be seen to ground the possibility of the moral form of life.

[13] See Chapter Eight for a discussion of this notion of an Ontological Imperative. See also p. 28, below.

[14] *CPrR*, p. 129, A 30.

[15] This is essential given Kant's conception of the nature of the human

realized through *our* being rational. Conscience then is reason personified and, as such, it is imbued with a 'desire' to *be* (to have its way) which it can only realize with our cooperation. In the dialogue it expresses this 'desire' with its question 'But would it be right (= practically valid) to behave according to your proposed maxim?' However, as we shall see, Desire has no natural capacity to act in accordance with maxims whose goals are unrelated to happiness. Thus if Conscience is to motivate Desire[16] it would have to present dutiful behaviour as the path to greater happiness.

However, in the nature of the case, this strategy is not open to it because the moral motivation to do what is right cannot consist of a desire for happiness. As we shall see in what follows, this stalemate leads to the emergence of the next element in the shadow model of moral causality, viz. a capacity to act freely which allows for the possibility of acting solely out of the thought of duty and thus without the motivation provided by any naturally occurring desire. We now return to the dialogue.

Reason: The practice of lying would necessarily self-destruct if universally practised. It is a practically invalid maxim.

Conscience: Reason has just indicated why, as I suspected, acting on your maxim would not be right. I charge you, Desire, not to act on your maxim. Do your duty and resist your inclination to lie.

Desire: Resist? I can't resist myself. I am Desire and I want only satisfaction. Reason said that if my maxim were followed *universally* it would self-destruct. As I weigh the alternatives for satisfaction presented to me by Reason I feel that, whether I lie or whether I do not, I will *eventually* end up in a dissatisfied state. But it seems to me that if I lie, I will initially, at least, get some satisfaction, before this lying of mine becomes common practice and eliminates itself as a means of obtaining

---

will as affected but not necessitated. It is not an *arbitrium brutum*, but an *arbitrium liberum*. See *CPR*, p. 465, A 534 B 562.

[16] Note that this portion of the dialogue is not intended to reflect Kant's own representation of *how* Reason works to persuade us to act morally. This is not his concern in the *CPrR* (the question there is how this persuasion is *possible* at all). It is only in the *FMM* in the four examples Kant gives to demonstrate how the Categorical Imperative is to be applied, that we get any idea of Reason's methods of persuasion. The dialogue here is an attempt to reconstruct this process, to see how Reason operates when it seeks to effect behaviour. The intention is to check the practicality of Kant's claim that Reason can be practical, by going through the procedure of solving a 'real-life' dilemma using Reason's methods.

satisfaction for a person who, like myself, is in financial straits.

At this stage, Desire, left to its own resources, would weigh up these alternatives and come down on one side or the other, depending on past experience.

<u>Conscience:</u> I can see that you really don't appreciate the character of the coercive power of my injunction to do your duty. I am not asking you to weigh the alternatives of either doing your duty or going against it, in terms of the satisfactions to be gained in either case. You have obviously missed the point. I am demanding of you that you do your duty simply because it is your duty to do what is right. It is just stupid to imagine that you could regard yourself as having done your duty if this were the result of your calculating that to do so would give you greater satisfaction, at least so far as *you* seem to understand satisfaction, that is, in terms of happiness.[17]

<u>Desire:</u> Now we seem to be getting somewhere. Is there another kind of satisfaction, other than happiness, which 'satisfies' those who do their duty? Tell me more. What is it like? Is it better than happiness?

<u>Conscience:</u> I am rather sorry I hinted at another source of satisfaction which a person like yourself might take as grist for your felicific mill. I'll admit however that those who do their duty do find themselves blessed with another kind of satisfaction called self-contentment.[18] However I cannot hasten quickly enough to add that this satisfaction cannot be sought as such. It only comes to those who do their duty solely in virtue of the fact that it is their duty. You will find that it cannot be obtained if it is sought as your goal. You cannot desire to obtain self-contentment, though of course you can 'desire' it, that is, consider it worth having.

<u>Desire:</u> Please talk sense. In my experience a desire is a desire. You can't 'want' something without wanting to obtain it.

<u>Conscience:</u> So you might think, but the very fact that I am talking to you about doing what is right as if you could do it without being motivated by any specific desire is sufficient proof to the contrary.[19]

---

[17] For Kant's arguments on this distinction between acting from duty and merely in accordance with duty, see *FMM*, p. 58 *ff*. BA 8 and *CPrR*, p. 180, A 127 and p. 188 A 144, the latter two drawing the distinction between morality and legality.

[18] See CPrR, p. 221, A 212 for an example of a uniquely moral component of a person's 'inner life'. See p. 16 above.

[19] This appears to be the essence of the argument from the fact of the moral law; from the reality of our awareness of an 'ought'. See *CPrR*, p. 143, A 56 and p. 157, A 81.

What you have to appreciate is that moral value is something you create *ex nihilo*. It is not a natural value like the happiness which you claim is the only value you know. It is created whenever a person acts on my injunctions through the recognition that to do so is right.

Desire: Hold on now. I can weigh *desires* to the turning of a hair, but I can't weigh 'desires' in my balance.[20] I don't like to be rude, but frankly I think you are wasting your breath on me. You have been addressing the wrong faculty. What you seem to need (if your appeal to duty is to awaken any response) is a faculty which 'seeks' self-contentment in a way analogous to my constant seeking after happiness. It would have to be a faculty which could somehow bring itself to choose to do what you call 'right' simply in virtue of the fact that it is right.

Conscience: I take my hat off to you. If through my injunction 'Do your duty' I could bring such a faculty into being, then morality—that kind of human behaviour which creates moral value—would be explicable. I can only conclude—transcendentally (if you will pardon the jargon)—that such a faculty must exist, since the form of life I serve (morality) exists.

If I then postulate such a faculty—call it Freedom—my call to duty would be intelligible.[21] You are quite right in regarding my appeal as unintelligible, so far as you are concerned. You are not free. I now recognize that it is not to you that my appeal is directed, but to that capacity in humankind which can, in virtue of its freedom, act according to the call of duty. The capacity to thus act 'on principle', to act without any ulterior motive, is what creates moral value and gives the person who so acts dignity.[22] In so far as people are free they can realize their inherent dignity by acting on principle. Reason is quite capable of testing the practical validity of the maxims which you (Desire) come up with, so long as I am present to put my question, and then Freedom (or perhaps we should say 'Humanity-in-its-freedom') can choose to create moral

---

[20] The point Desire is making here is that these phenomena—duty, self-contentment, etc.—are not part of its experience or (personification aside) not part of the experience or inner life of a person who is without a sense of moral values.

[21] This argument from morality to freedom is explicit and is frequently repeated in the *CPrR*. See, for example, p. 235, A 238-239 in the discussion of the postulates. Morality, involving an independence from the world of sense, presupposes freedom. This is also expressed in terms of freedom being the *ratio essendi*—the logical ground—of morality. *CPrR*, p. 119, A 5, also pp. 140-141, A 52-53

[22] See FMM, pp. 92-93, BA 77-78. Dignity, another uniquely moral phenomenon, is considered to be an outgrowth of self-respect. For further treatment see pp. 123 *ff.*, below.

value by acting only on those maxims which are practically valid. (*At this point in the dialogue the shadow model of moral causality has been fully illustrated.*) To sum up: the causal 'explanation' of moral behaviour involves 1) a rational stimulus (the recognition of the practical validity of a proposed maxim of action) which produces 2) a sense of obligation (a 'desire' to act in accordance with the proposed maxim in order to be consistent, to do what is right, to *be* good). However, we lack any natural desire to fulfill this obligation and consequently, if moral behaviour is to be regarded as possible we must assume 3) that we possess a capacity to fulfill the obligation through a free act of will, an exercise which brings about 4) a feeling of self-contentment (a 'satisfaction') which is identical with that sense of dignity which comes with the knowledge that one has autonomously directed one's behaviour with reference to the rational maxim which initiated this sequence of moral behaviour.

The factor which makes this explanation an 'explanation'—a shadow only—is the notion of freedom and its exercise. Desire has a question or two about this capacity which Conscience will now be allowed to struggle with as its answers raise issues which will play a large part in the following chapters.

Desire: You haven't forgotten that this freedom can cut both ways? A person can freely choose to follow my maxims even though they turn out to be practically invalid.[23]

Conscience: I haven't forgotten. People can choose to be evil. Negative moral values can be created as well. This is the price that being free extracts from a person.

Desire: And people still have dignity if they choose to be evil?

Conscience: Yes. They are responsible[24] for their actions, whether they choose to be good or evil. The measure of their dignity when they choose the evil alternative is that, if they are caught and convicted of wrong-doing, they demand to be punished, although you undoubtedly would want them to escape the punishment. However they cannot give up the birthright their freedom confers upon them. Not to punish people is to deny them their dignity as human beings. It amounts to treating them as things which cannot control their behaviour.

Desire: So, why then should people choose the good rather than the

---

[23] This is the problem that Kant tackles in *RWL*, especially Book One.

[24] But see pp. 112 *ff.* below, where responsible behaviour is discussed in connection with agent-naturalism.

evil course of action? Clearly you want (if that term makes sense when anyone but I says it) them to choose to do what is right. You presumably see greater worth resting with the choice of good than with the choice of evil. But if their status as beings capable of morality is conferred upon them by their capacity freely to choose between right and wrong courses of action, do they not retain their dignity, their self-respect, their moral worth, whichever alternative they choose? The greater worth that lies with the good choice is not, it seems, a result of this choice being necessary for human dignity but rather it is a function of your own 'preference' for good over evil. What lies behind this preference? What is good about being good? Why should Humanity-in-its-freedom want to be good?

Conscience: From your point of view, where all action is a function of desire, that certainly is a problem. For when you ask why a person should choose good over evil, you are asking why Humanity-in-its-freedom should *want* to identify with Reason and so act only upon practically valid (universalizable) principles, and you are naturally curious (in terms of the only motivational structure you know) as to what exactly is to be gained by such a person. You, after all, cannot appreciate what 'good' means for a person if it does not relate to the satisfaction of desire, nor evil if not to unsatisfied desire. Nor can you understand what satisfaction means if it is not cashed in terms of happiness.

Humanity-in-its-freedom, however, is determined neither by desire nor by my pleas *viz,* that it act as the categorical voice of Reason demands. Humanity-in-its-freedom is not a faculty which can be dictated to. As free, this faculty (personified) is subject only to an ontological imperative.[25] Humanity-in-its-freedom must exercise this freedom *in order to be* , and there are only two choices: this *persona* can either be indulgent (as I would like to put it), seeking prudently or imprudently the satisfaction of its desires as they occur, or it can be rational, acting only on practically valid maxims.[26] Now it has no 'preferences' in making this choice, in the sense in which you understand this term. This *persona* is not predisposed to be indulgent or rational by any feelings which it may experience. It is entirely without dispositions, preferences, indeed, without a character at all. Instead it creates positive or negative moral value through the free choices it makes. Without predispositions,

---

[25] See Chapter Eight.
[26] In the *CPrR* this choice between two clearcut options is expressed as a choice between succumbing to inclination and therefore realizing only the immediate objects of desire or resisting inclination and following Reason's way of duty, thereby realizing virtue. See pp. 180 *ff.*, A 126 *ff.*

without inclinations to tell it what to do, it cannot avoid acting autonomously and this is the source of its capacity to create moral values. Thus the only question it can ask itself is: 'What ought I to be?', not as you might have thought: 'What do I want to be?' The former question can only be answered by answering the ontologically prior question: 'What am I?' since only in terms of what the *persona*—Humanity-in-its-freedom—is, can it choose what it ought to be. Its answer to this question is that it is whatever it wills itself to be and that therefore it always retains its freedom to be what it wills. It can create a rational or indulgent character for itself but its character is always being created afresh by each act of will.

Now that you have grasped the ontological circumstances of Humanity-in-its-freedom, I will rephrase your question: 'Why should Humanity-in-its-freedom want to be good?' What sense does it make to say that this *persona* ought to behave as Reason (categorically) dictates and why does it not make sense to say that it ought to be indulgent?

Desire: Yes, why is Humanity-in-its-freedom obliged to be good, to follow Reason? Why is it not obliged to be happy, to follow my lead? (Please note that I did not ask why it is not obliged to be evil, as if seeking happiness were evil!)

Conscience: How patient I am. I understand what you are on about. And I simply refuse to take offence at your quite delightful consistency in always equating goodness with happiness.

Once again let me spell out my position: people do not become happy by being good, they become good, period. Whether or not they should also experience happiness or unhappiness as a consequence of their decision to be good is a purely contingent matter and it is quite irrelevant to their choosing to be good. So too with the choice to be evil. Evil people may or may not be happy. Their decision to be evil is not a decision to be happy or unhappy but to be evil. Ontological commitments have only ontological consequences.

Desire: But what about self-contentment? Surely this is experienced as an emotional "plus" and would therefore prompt Humanity-in-its-freedom to choose to be good?

Conscience: There is also an emotional "plus", as you put it, associated with being evil. Consider Milton's Satan. But, to repeat myself, these are not the factors which prompt ontological commitments. They are not (and cannot be) causal factors in what is, by definition, a free act. They are irrelevant because they are contingent side-effects. Good and evil must be understood as ontological values, brought into being by ontological commitments. They don't just happen, they are *created* through free choices.

Desire: Let me ask my question again in your words: why should Humanity-in- its-freedom choose to be good rather than evil?

Conscience: The answer is complicated. You know that your desires do not arise spontaneously. They are always traceable to some empirical stimulus which aroused them. Reason, by comparison, although it can on occasions be activated by desire, can also engage in spontaneous activity, activity that derives from its own nature.[27] Its spontaneity is thus a mark of the autonomous or self-governing aspect of its nature. This self-governing aspect of reasoning is exemplified in the fact that reasoning itself sets the standard for whether or not it is reasoning.[28]

---

[27] See *CPR*, p. 473, A 548 B 576, for the perfect spontaneity of reason in creating its own order. See also *FMM*, p. 106, BA 108.

[28] When reasoning takes place properly (and, in a sense, it cannot fail to operate properly), this proper reasoning is marked by the fact that the conclusions arrived at *follow* from the premises on which they are based. What does this 'following' amount to? Well, what is followed, what is adhered to, are the rules which determine whether an argument is valid or not. And where do these rules come from? They are based on Reason's capacity to recognize instances of class-inclusion. For example, in the famous syllogism—All men are mortal; Socrates is a man; therefore Socrates is mortal—Reason sees that, since men are included within the class of mortals, and Socrates is included within the class of men, then Socrates falls within the class of mortals as well. In diagrammatic terms, Reason can see that the smallest circle is contained in the largest:

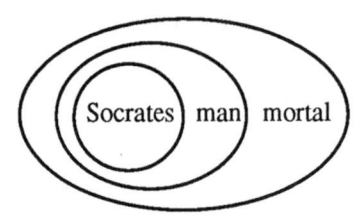

If Reason couldn't see these relationships it couldn't reason. Reasoning is just seeing relationships of class-inclusion and seeing these relationships is reasoning. This ability to see—in diagrammatic terms, that one circle is *inside* another—is so basic that Reason cannot help seeing such relationships wherever it looks. This explains why its spontaneous tendency to *universalize* relationships (Is it all right for me to lie? Is it all right for *everyone* to lie?) is always guided by the very rule which constitutes its activity *and* its validity. Reasoning is thus always valid, i.e. *proceeds in accordance with its own rule*, because Reason cannot fail to see (again, using the diagrammatic model) that one circle is inside another. So-called 'invalid' reasoning is always a function of the fact that 'the circles' have not been properly drawn, or in other words, that the terms involved have not been clearly defined in relation to

This may sound odd, but all spontaneous self-governing phenomena are odd in having this reflexive feature. You could say that Reason's activity was 'motivated' by its own nature, its tendency to universalize. Now let us return to your question: 'Why should a person choose to do what is right (good) rather than what is wrong (evil)?' or as I would prefer to put it: 'Why should a person choose to live as if they were Reason personified?' Since doing what is right is to be understood in terms of acting according to universalizable maxims, maxims which, when followed, are not practically invalid, my version of the question clarifies the problem which your question raises. For Reason, were it an agent, would always act on practically valid lines. To be specific, were Reason an agent it would always ask (following its tendency to universalize): 'Would this action which I contemplate doing be possible (practically valid) if everyone acted as I intend to act, or would it self-destruct if universally practised?'

Why then should Humanity-in-its-freedom ask this question of itself, and like Reason personified, act only on practically valid maxims? The answer is that Humanity-in-its-freedom is—if I may put it this way—*pure* spontaneity: it must will in order to be. But it is under no compulsion to will to be indulgent or rational, although it must will to be one or the other. Now this pure spontaneity which characterizes Humanity-in-its-freedom would have no value or interest if it made its ontological commitment randomly. Unless it chose deliberately to be rational or indulgent the value created by its choice—moral value—would vanish. Thus the choice it makes must be made deliberately, that is, according to some principle. Furthermore, if it simply *made up* this principle it would, in effect, be acting randomly and hence would not be seen as a creator of moral value. The choice is free, but unless it makes a difference whether the choice is made one way or the other, for good or for evil, then the choice cannot create moral value. What could this

---

each other. So when I point out that an argument is invalid (that it doesn't follow) I always point to the fact that a given term is not in fact related to the other term in the way suggested by the argument. It is the facts contained in the premises of an argument not the mechanics of reasoning, that are incorrect. In other words, I would never suggest to someone that his or her reasoning was invalid on the grounds that, while a given circle was drawn inside a larger circle, he or she somehow managed to see it outside the larger circle. That is assumed to be impossible. What is possible is that the thing under consideration does not actually belong in the circle as believed (e.g. if Socrates were not, in fact, a man.) This explanation accords with Kant's idea in the Analytic of the *CPR* of how Reason operates in its function as Understanding in the sphere of General Logic.

principle of moral choice be? Since it must motivate an ontological choice, it can only be an ontological principle and, for an agent, the only[29] ontological motive is to be what you essentially are. But what is the essential nature of a free agent? On the one hand it cannot be the agent's freedom since this aspect of its agency only places it under the onus of choosing. Its essential nature as free does not indicate which alternative to choose. But, on the other hand, the essential nature of a free agent must involve the agent's freedom since such an agent is characterized solely in terms of the freedom of its agency.

Now I have already pointed out that if a free agent expresses its freedom randomly, this exercise of its freedom would not create a moral value since it would not create a characteristic pattern of willing which could be thought of as good or evil. And I also said that the characteristic pattern of willing—the person's character, for short—did not, and could not, determine the continuance of the pattern it displays: the agent is always free to alter its characteristic pattern of willing. The exercise of freedom is only significant, it only creates moral value, when it is expressed in a series of willings which are consistent enough for a characteristic pattern of either good or evil (rational or indulgent) willing to emerge.[30] So it follows that the free activity of willing which creates such patterns will derive its consistency from the free adoption by agents of either the principle of indulgent behaviour (in terms of which each action which they subsequently take will be a foregone conclusion as soon as a given desire makes itself manifest) or a principle based on the categorical advice of Reason (in which each action is tested for its practical validity before being enacted).

If then Humanity-in-its-freedom must act upon its ontological imperative—be what you essentially are—which principle of action ought it to adopt in order to obey this imperative?

Now I say that if it adopts the principle of indulgence it, in a sense, limits its freedom to this single act of will, for by definition the adoption

---

[29] But see Chapter Eight, below, where a second ontological motive is suggested.

[30] This is true only when we are considering moral worth "in the judgment of men who can appraise themselves and the strength of their maxims only by the ascendency which they win over their sensuous nature in time." (*RWL*, p. 43, A 51-52 B 55) That is, when we are summing up the character of a person, we consider his or her actions (retrospectively) to see whether a pattern has developed. But each individual act, in which freedom is exercised (for the moral option) is good in itself, independently of what sort of choices went before or will come after. It is this independence of each choice that makes change possible.

of the principle of indulgence precludes any further free choices. But Humanity-in-its-freedom is essentially free. It cannot give up its freedom in this fashion and remain true to its nature. Thus from an ontological point of view (accepting the primacy of the ontological imperative) Humanity-in-its-freedom ought to choose to be rational since such a choice involves giving up neither the freedom to oppose Desire, when Reason warns that the following of a given Desire would result in a practically invalid action, nor the freedom to seek satisfaction if Reason rules that such satisfaction is permitted.[31] Nor indeed does the adoption of the rational principle of behaviour rule out, simply in virtue of its initial adoption, the occasional indulgence. It only rules out consistent indulgence on pain of ceasing to display that characteristic pattern of rational willing that marks a person as essentially good. To be what you are is to be ontologically consistent, to be right in the sense of being in line with one's *self* (which must mean one's essential nature). This is what *being* good means.

Desire: You seem to be suggesting that to opt for a life in accordance with Reason's dictates is to opt to be more truly oneself, to live more in line with one's real nature as a free being. When you say to Humanity-in-its-freedom: "Do your duty." you are really saying: "Create, by an act of will, the identity for yourself most in keeping with your capacity for freedom." You are saying: "Start acting on principle so that you can *be* someone you can respect, someone you can ontologically live with. Unless you do, you will be nothing but a part of Nature, as much subject to desire as Desire is to those natural occurrences which stimulate it. However you can—in your freedom—become what you essentially are, what you were ontologically 'meant' to be." Now I can appreciate the strength of this ontological appeal. In appealing to Humanity as free, you appeal to the human capacity to create a new, harmonious (which is to say, practically valid) order of existence. As such you treat this *persona* of humanity as a god, one who has not as yet realized its creative potential but can do so simply through an act of will. But, with this splendid vision before its eyes, will this *persona* perhaps be blind to the content of the principles it acts on in order to bring this vision into being? I mention this because my world—the world in which happiness is the be-all and end-all—has suffered terribly at the hands of people acting "on principle". You certainly don't want people to identify with a capacity (Reason) which cannot itself distinguish between happiness-producing principles and their opposite, do you? Or do you really mean to

---

[31] There are difficulties with this argument. See pp. 40 *ff.*, below.

stick to your guns and insist that a good will (which equals the decision to act solely for the sake of duty—whatever the consequences) is the only good thing, *the* value in comparison with which happiness is an irrelevant contingency.

Conscience: I'm afraid I must, as you put it, 'stick to my guns'. No one can take any pleasure (moral pleasure that is, the only sort worth having) in the sight of a person visited by happiness who is not also morally good.[32] However, I am not against happiness. There is nothing wrong with it *per se* but, obviously, if the happiness resulting from an action were to be regarded as the standard of worth by which human behaviour was ultimately to be judged, we would have to know, *a priori*, what principles of behaviour would maximize our happiness if we were to seek happiness "on principle". And Reason, which supplies people with their principles, cannot say *a priori* what the consequences in terms of happiness of the application of its principles (which could be no more than the counsels of prudence) might be.[33] Reason can only determine *a priori* whether a principle would be practically valid or invalid. It is thus able to distinguish what actions are permitted, but, of course, it cannot say whether such actions would result in a greater or lesser amount of happiness in the world if they were followed. It can only guarantee that people who confine their behaviour to that which is permitted by Reason will experience self-contentment, they will know that they are good people, people whose behaviour is determined by Reason.[34]

Desire: So, if I understand you, you have no objection to people finding happiness incidentally, so to speak, so long as happiness is not what motivates them?

Conscience: That's right. A moral person accepts his or her lot so far as happiness is concerned.

The dialogue may end at this point. The main features of the shadow model of moral causality are now before us. We have been told what it is to be good and how—according to the shadow model of moral causality—this state can be achieved. From the point of view of the original model (based on natural causal relationships) the shadow model does not really explain how moral behaviour is possible and, since the original model sets the standard of intelligibility for an explanation, it would seem to be something of a mystery that the shadow model of moral causality is intelligible at all. In the following chapter we will try to explain this mystery.

---

[32] Cf. p. 4-5, above.
[33] See *FMM*, pp. 57-58, BA 6-7 and p. 77, BA 45-46.
[34] *ibid.*, p. 58, BA 7

CHAPTER THREE

REFLEXIVE DECISION-MAKING

I

In the last chapter the dialogue form was used to introduce the shadow model of moral causality. In the dialogue, Desire, as the defender of natural causality, indicates that it does not really understand how moral behaviour is possible. It does not understand how Reason can be practical because, at bottom, it does not know what the free exercise of the will amounts to. For Desire, the shadow model of moral causality is unintelligible because natural causality is somehow suspended and freedom enters in its place as a kind of *deus ex machina* which permits moral behaviour. Desire's frank puzzlement raises the question which we wish to answer in this chapter.

The question is: given that Desire has a right to be puzzled—a right to challenge the intelligibility of the shadow model—why is it that we apparently understand Conscience when it expounds the shadow model? Why do we think we understand moral causality? Is Desire simply being naive, or are we being less than frank? Do we understand freedom? It would appear that we must since we talk about it quite easily, and yet we can certainly appreciate Desire's puzzlement. We are in two minds on this matter. How did this situation come about?

We can begin to answer this question by explaining why it was that the dialogue form originally recommended itself as the easiest way in which to set out the structure of that form of life which constitutes morality. Consider a description of some moral conflict as it is experienced from a first person point of view. (The description emphasizes the fact that the person experiencing the inner conflict is aware of his or her thoughts and feelings in that special complex mode of awareness known as self-consciousness.)

I am aware of the fact that I want something and that this desire is urging me to act upon it. I am aware of wondering if it would be right to go ahead and follow this desire. I am aware of being aware of a feeling of uneasiness about just acting on this desire without considering what might happen if I do. I feel myself wanting to do x and also wanting to give doing x some thought before I do anything, and I am aware of myself as aware of these conflicting desires. I am aware of myself as wanting to be free of this conflict. I am aware of a need to decide one way or the other. I begin to think about how I would feel if I did x. I am aware that I would be satisfied but also uneasy in myself, if x is wrong. I am aware of this thought. I think then of whether doing x is actually wrong. I am aware of thinking that it would be. I am aware of wondering whether I care whether I think it is wrong or not, since it is just thinking. I am aware of thinking that it isn't just thinking since this same thinking will still be with me if I act against it. I think of this. (Finally I either care or I don't care, with the result that I act one way or the other.)

Clearly the only thing that limits the reflexive complexity of this stream of consciousness is the impenetrable factor of how much I care about the shape of my life: how much store I set on the two values of, on the one hand, satisfying my inclinations and, on the other, feeling morally ill at ease. It would seem that there are only two ways in which this question of how much I care about these values can be resolved: one way is by letting my past experience decide for me; the other is actively to decide which value is to count as pre-eminent with me.

It is worth noting at the outset of this discussion that adopting the first, or passive, option could still be construed as constituting a decision which I make, in the sense that adopting this passive stance could well involve the explicit recognition that I cannot, in fact, ignore the counsels of my past experience, since I must always live with them. It is simply my nature as a self-conscious being to be aware of how I feel about what has happened to me in the past and hence to have at hand, at all times, an evolving standard in terms of which I am able to judge the viability of any two conflicting ways of behaving. Explicitly recognizing this aspect of my nature and accepting it amounts to a decision to trust myself, to trust in my innate capacity to judge where my well-being lies.[1]

(This sense of well-being will not be easily characterized as either happiness or moral self-contentment. It is an ontological value (*well-being*) derived from being/acting in tune with one's feelings. But more of what this amounts to in a moment.)

Now, by contrast, the second, or active option, takes it for granted that

---

[1] Of course I might behave in this way naturally, i.e. without the explicit recognition that I am depending on a natural decision-making capacity when I 'make' my decisions by following my judgmental feelings.

decision-making is an option which we must explicitly adopt. It assumes that the alternatives before us (that one can either be happy and satisfy one's inclinations or be content and do what is right) are incommensurable and therefore cannot be weighed in the same balance, with the result that one must actively choose between them if one is to act. But as we are by now aware, being faced with this choice between doing what is right or doing what makes one happy allows for the possibility of creating a new kind of value, namely, a moral value. And this Kantian view carries with it the implication that no explanation (in terms of natural causality) can be given for why the choice—whether to be good or to be indulgent (= happy)—should go one way rather than the other. In other words the choice must be a *free* choice if it is to create a moral value. Thus the second option assumes that the reflexive monologue is not capable of being resolved on natural lines. It assumes that the natural vacillation between the two alternatives would go on forever, that the two alternatives are like two obstinate people who cannot compromise (since there is no common ground between them) nor give up their individual claims to dominate without (they consider) annihilating themselves in the process.

Therefore any analysis of the second option necessarily requires the postulation of a third person to adjudicate as to which of the two contenders will be left in possession of the field. In addition to this, the second option cannot assume that this third person could decide between them on natural grounds. Thus, for example, the decision cannot follow from some predisposition (on the part of the adjudicator) to prefer happiness to being good or *vice versa*. The role of the adjudicator is to *create* a preference (a value) by choosing one way or the other.

However, if the decision is not to be based on some natural predisposition of the free agent, this means that the decision must be grounded in some principle which is unintelligible from the point of view of natural causality. Thus, in choosing, the adjudicator cannot give reasons for its choice other than: 'I did it because I wanted to' or 'I did it because it was right'. In other words, the adjudicator cannot answer the question: 'But why did you choose the one rather than the other?' except through declaring (creating) a preference. (One natural way to read this declaration is as a free act of identification on the part of the adjudicator with either Reason or Desire as the dominant part of his or her personality.)

This 'refusal' to explain the choice also has a counterpart in the case of the first option. On that option, decisions can only be explained in terms of the natural role which past experience has in making choices. Thus people are simply aware of the way that they, as human beings with a history, feel about the two alternatives and this awareness constitutes their 'decision'. In trusting to their feelings about the alternatives presented by Reason and Desire, they are being true to themselves in the sense of acknowledging that these judgmental feelings, which have arisen as a result of their reflection on the situation, are definitive of their being as agents. They have no sense of the choice being made for them,[2] but also no sense of how they make the choice beyond that of having presented the options to themselves in order to see how they feel about them.

This then, on the first option, is what choosing amounts to. Choosing here is fully explicable in terms of our natural capacity to assess how we feel. And as the chooser we accept the imputation that the choice was ours, in the sense of stemming from our own reflexive capacity to decide. It was we who reflected on the options and, as a result, came to feel a certain way concerning them.

On the second option the 'refusal' to explain one's choice is interpreted as a sign that the choice was a free choice. By this it is meant that agents do not discover how they feel through some natural process of reflective judgment, but rather decide to identify with either Reason or Desire, in order to become that sort of person. Instead of discovering what they are like (i.e. how they feel and thus what they are going to do) through considering their feelings (as in the first option), they regard themselves as creating what they are to be through their decision, creating their moral self (as either a good or an indulgent willer) out of nothing, with no reference to any natural predispositions. Kant saw this kind of completely autonomous choosing as definitive of moral decision-making.[3]

When people proceed according to the second option they regard the consequences of their choice—in terms of the happiness that may or may not occur in their life (or the lives of others)—as not affecting the moral value created though their good (or indulgent) willing. Why is this the case? On the first option, the consequences which follow upon the decisions people make play a part in determining their future conduct, because the consequences of their decisions add to the fund of experience upon which the person draws when making subsequent decisions. How-

---

[2] That is, no sense of being passive, of being externally determined.

[3] See *RWL*, p. 40, A 45 B 48: "Man *himself* must make or have made himself into whatever, in a moral sense, whether good or evil, he is or is to become."

ever, on the second option, the consequences of the decisions people make in a given situation cannot affect their future conduct. Because the will is free on each occasion that it is exercised, it cannot be affected by the consequences of past choices.

The phenomenon of being reflexively aware when we choose is thus capable of being interpreted as the ground of two quite different conceptions of human agency. On the first interpretation, reflection is regarded as a natural procedure through which our past experience has the opportunity to affect our present state of mind. If it is not interfered with, this procedure produces viable conduct, which is to say it produces that sense of well-being which comes from being in tune with our own feelings when we act.

The other interpretation of this phenomenon, along the lines suggested in the second option, is the interpretation that regards an agent as capable of morality, a form of life which involves the creation of a new kind of value and which assumes (by way of an explanation of its possibility) a shadow version of causality with freedom of the will as its core concept. This second interpretation sees reflection—our capacity for reflexive awareness—as presenting a problem. It sees the reflexive self as being presented with separate faculties—Desire and Reason—which have different goals and with which it must somehow deal, somehow organize and control, through exercising the power freely to choose between them. If it does not take charge, no one will and chaos will result. A choice therefore must be made.

On the second interpretation, the fact that we are reflexively aware places upon us the direct obligation to choose between Desire and Reason. Apart from making such a choice, there is no way to resolve the conflict between Desire's wants and Reason's dictates. Thus the choice we make will create a moral value (of goodness or self-indulgence depending on whether we value Reason over Desire or vice versa).

The problem, on the second interpretation, is how this choosing is to be accomplished—once we become aware that we are under a moral obligation to make such a choice. Thus a moral obligation is simply an obligation to create a moral value and this obligation arises, and can arise, only from the neutral perspective provided by our capacity to be reflexively aware. If we have the idea that for action to ensue, this neutral perspective must be overcome and if, for whatever reasons, we have the idea that our feelings (our judgmental feelings) cannot be decisive in this matter, we are then forced to the conclusion that we ourselves must freely decide what course we are to take. On this second interpetation then, the question of *how* this choosing is to be accomplished naturally occupies centre-stage and it is at this point that the reason why Chapter Two assumed the form of a dialogue becomes apparent.

Once our mental capacities, our faculties, have emerged as distinct personalities—Reason and Desire—then the question of how a given faculty comes to gain ascendancy can only be answered by taking ordinary personal relations as a model. For this is the only model we have for settling conflicts between mutually exclusive interests. Thus if Bill wants x and Mary wants y and each can only have what each wants if Tom wants it too, they will ask Tom to decide who should be allowed to have what he or she wants. Now Tom can expect Mary and Bill to persuade him with any means at their disposal, in order to bring him around to their particular points of view. Their natural strategy will be to convince Tom that he is actually like them and therefore should, by nature (i.e. on ontological grounds), follow their lead. Mary will say to Tom that he must acknowledge that a life without happiness is not worth having, Bill that unprincipled heteronomous behaviour is beneath Tom's dignity as a free agent, etc., etc.

However there is a problem in applying such efforts to personified faculties: by definition, Humanity-in-its-freedom (the Adjudicator) has no personal nature to appeal to. The capacity to choose must be kept characterless, when personified, in order to ensure that its freedom to choose is not influenced by any predispositions. This consideration was, in fact, already making things awkward at one stage in the dialogue when Reason, in the form of Conscience, put forward a dubious argument to the effect that Humanity-in-its-freedom ought to choose to be rational since such a choice was somehow more in keeping with its essential nature.[4] Conscience is not exactly convincing when it tries to maintain that Humanity-in-its-freedom has a specific nature such that a particular choice can either be in accord with, or in opposition to, that nature. It is worth reviewing this argument in order to see precisely where the flaw in it lies.

The fundamental difficulty that Conscience wrestles with is how Humanity-in-its-freedom can exercise its free choice in such a way as to give moral value to its choices. It is agreed that random choices do not create moral value. To create moral value, our choices must be based on a principle. Now even if we assume, for the sake of the argument, that the free adoption of a principle upon which to base one's choice is the fundamental creative act upon which depends the very possibility of

---

[4] See pp. 30*ff*, above.

moral value, a difficulty remains: how are we to determine which principle has been adopted? Just why this is a problem may be seen by considering the following points.

From a third-person point of view, only an established characteristic pattern of willing (one showing that most of the things a given person does are either indulgent or dutiful) could reveal that the exercise of that person's capacity freely to choose was being based on some principle and not being exercised randomly. However, from a first-person point of view, I recognize, in so far as I regard myself as free, that my past choices have not made me good, or self-indulgent: only my present choice can do this. The essence of being free is to regard the future as being composed of options which are open to me, whatever I may have done in the past. From a third-person point of view, I am a certain sort of person, judged to be such on the basis of a characteristic pattern of behaviour which I have exhibited in the past. From my own point of view, I am not confined by my past behaviour to being always a certain sort of person. From this perspective, only when I exercise my freedom do I gain, albeit briefly, a character.

This means that the argument in the dialogue—which assumed that displaying a certain pattern of willing (an indulgent pattern) restricted one's freedom more than displaying the alternative pattern—though it might make some sense from a third-person perspective, makes none when considered from a first-person perspective. From the latter point of view the choice facing me is always an open one. I can never commit myself to being indulgent on future occasions. As free, I cannot—either through a series of choices or through one 'great' choice—establish a character for myself which will somehow serve to deprive me of my freedom to be indulgent or dutiful in the future. I am only as good, or indulgent, as my last choice makes me. The moral value that a person creates through the choice that they make only characterizes them until they are faced with their next (moral) choice.[5]

We are now in a position to add a further complexity to the second interpretation of the nature of reflexive decision-making. As we have already noted, on this second interpretation it is natural to treat desire and reason from a third-person standpoint, as if they were individuals separate from myself (my reflexive self). However it now appears that it is equally

---

[5] This would seem to be the rationale behind the idea of the death-bed confession, a necessarily final choice, epitomized in the traditional Catholic practice of making a good death (see, e.g. *Brideshead Revisited* by Evelyn Waugh).

natural that I who must choose between them—I as a free agent—should also come to be seen from a third-person point of view. This is because the choice that 'I' make (as a free agent) immediately becomes like the choice of some third party from the point of view of the reflexive self who is aware of the direction of this choice. In other words, my exercise of my own agency is alienated from me when this choice is considered reflexively: I become aware of 'my' choice as not really constitutive of my being (now) since—in my freedom— what I am (dutiful or indulgent) can only be determined through my next choice. Thus I find my capacity for reflexive consciousness always reduces me to the position of a passive spectator, occupying a first person perspective from which I note what 'I' am like as I make my decisions.

On the second interpretation I become what I am (good or self-indulgent) by choosing. I then, as a self who is reflexively aware of 'my' action, immediately distance myself from the moral value of this newly created way of behaving by becoming aware of the choice as 'mine' (the person I was at the time) and, in doing so, I simultaneously open the question of what I (the reflexive self) am really like. What I am really like can only be determined by my next decision and so on *ad infinitum*. The complete passivity, the sense of detachment, which pertains to the self—as identified with my capacity to be reflexively aware—means that I cannot be 'like' anything, so long as I am reflexively aware. Under this interpretation of reflexive consciousness, I have a character only from the third-person point of view, never from the first-person perspective. In Kantian terms I can be attributed virtue as *virtus phaenomenon*, never as *virtus noumenon*.[6] This is how it must be if the moral options which are grounded in my freedom are to remain intact. Moral options call for a free choice.

So the metamoral dilemma remains: we have no rational way of deciding whether we should follow the promptings of Desire or the dictates of Reason, so long as we insist that this decision be free. This is why the argument which Conscience used to answer the question of why Humanity-in-its-freedom should choose to be good was not convincing.

We noted above that the naturalistic interpretation of choosing is also based on the phenomenon of reflexive consciousness. But, by contrast, it finds within reflexive consciousness itself an intelligible basis for decision-making. It finds this in our first-person awareness of a balance of feelings with which we—even as reflexively aware—naturally identify. We will present our arguments for this view in the following section.

---

[6] See *RWL*, p. 42-43 A 49 B 51.

II

The above considerations have shown how reflexive consciousness may be seen as the ground of two quite different views concerning decision-making. In order to understand how it is that these quite divergent views can be grounded in the same phenomenon we need to consider the phenomenology of reflexive consciousness in more detail. Since this is not entirely familiar territory, it will perhaps be best to launch these considerations by describing some other modes of consciousness which are more familiar and which can be related to reflexive states in such a way as to make these latter states more accessible. The first of these is

Passive Absorption

This is a state of consciousness which I describe retrospectively as one in which I was *absorbed* in what I was doing. When I am absorbed in some activity, I may describe myself—again retrospectively—as having been lost in what I was doing. This is a familiar experience whose paradigm is being lost in a book. What gets 'lost' in such states is my reflexive awareness, my sense of being aware of myself and what I am up to. When I am passively absorbed, I cannot, at the same time, describe my state of mind because this state of mind lacks a conscious perspective, i.e. it is not a *reflexive* state. Only when I 'come back to myself', i.e. again become reflexively aware, can I describe my previous state as one of absorption. In our daily lives, we are continually shifting back and forth between these two modes of consciousness, though we often experience a 'mixed mode' which we could designate as either

Active Absorption or *Active Reflection.*

In such a state I am absorbed in something and yet my sense of what I am up to is not far away, so to speak. This is my characteristic state of mind when I am working on some project. I am absorbed in what I am doing, but not to the extent that I cease to be aware of what I am doing. I maintain my sense of direction in such a state, as a kind of 'hovering presence' which intervenes whenever what I am doing ceases to be relevant to the task at hand. This is what working amounts to from a phenomenological point of view. In such a state I am *actively* absorbed in what I am doing because while I am absorbed in my task, I am continually reflecting upon whether what I am doing is relevant to the end which I have in view. My capacity to be aware of what I am up to is thus practically engaged, in contrast to that state of reflexive awareness which we shall call

Passive   Reflection.

In this mode of consciousness we are aware of our state of mind as if we were a third person, a spectator. This is the state which we often experience when we 'come back to ourselves' after having been passively absorbed. Having been lost in a book, for example, I come back to 'reality' and realize that I am feeling chilly and rather hungry. From this point of view I can make observations about myself as if I were someone else.

This mode of consciousness is of special interest in any discussion of decision-making, for when I am in such a 'detached' state I can see myself quite dispassionately and hence with a mind that is quite open to any options for future behaviour which may present themselves. I can describe myself from a third-person point of view as someone who is seeking such and such a goal or satisfaction and I can—from this passively reflexive perspective—see that I have a choice as to whether I shall continue what I was doing, viz. reading the book or, alternatively, forget the book, warm up and find myself a snack. From the passively reflexive standpoint I can observe how I feel about these options. It is then a standpoint which allows us to stand back and weigh up alternatives.

Can these distinctions help us to explain why our capacity to be reflexively aware permits both the natural and the moral conceptions of decision-making to exist? In particular, can they explain how moral decision-making comes to be superimposed upon our natural decision-making procedure?

We will begin our discussion of this question with a reminder of the absolute distinction which Kant insisted must be drawn between moral value and utility value. Kant would not have accepted any interpretation of the place of morality in our lives that involved seeing moral worth as a special case of utility value. When moral decision-making is superimposed on natural decision-making it creates an entirely new kind of value—moral value—which cannot be reduced to a utility value even if moral value were to be given the status of the fundamental or supreme kind of utility value. Kant had at least two objections to this way of dealing with moral value. In the first place, Kant held that something powers can only be employed hypothetically, that is, used only to find the best means of maximizing an already given end (happiness). On such an interpretation we are simply natural creatures, totally subject to desire with no values other than happiness with which to underwrite the worth of our existence. Kant finds this unacceptable. If we agree with Kant that this notion of a person's dignity is an intelligible notion representing a value that is very important to our conception of ourselves as human beings, we will have to consider whether there is a place for it in a naturalistic interpretation of human behaviour. Can the natural value, happiness, be deepened or transformed in some way so that it can explain the special place which the notion of dignity has in our lives? We will consider this question in Chapter Seven.

A second reason for Kant's opposition to the reduction of moral value to utility value is his belief that we can have no reliable instinct for happiness,[7] no inbuilt capacity to judge what course of action will maximize our well-being. This is because he allows no place for feelings, not even disinterested feelings, as valid guides to our conduct. In a way this is surprising, since he insisted that disinterested feelings are to be regarded as a valid basis for making *aesthetic* judgments.[8] However, unlike Hume[9] for example, he did not think that such feelings could play this role in moral judgments. In the moral sphere Kant regards disinterested feelings as simply inclinations and therefore as tainted with self-interest.

Just why Kant took this view of disinterested feelings in relation to moral judgments can be understood in the light of the modes of consciousness which we have recently distinguished. When we are in a passively reflexive mode of consciousness any feelings we may have are experienced from a third-person perspective and thus in a disinterested fashion. They therefore have a *prima facie* claim to be reliable guides for our conduct. To illustrate the nature of this *prima facie* claim we can ask of Kant: would he acknowledge a role for these feelings in non-moral judgments? Would feelings be a legitimate guide in that area of optional activities which we designate as 'permissible' i.e., activities passed by the Categorical Imperative as practically valid?

Suppose, then, a situation in which I am engaged in a permissible activity and the desire to engage in another permissible activity arises.

---

[7] *FMM*, pp. 56-57, BA 4-5.
[8] See *CJ*, CaJ pp. 41-89, A 3-73, B 3-74.
[9] cf. Hume who drew this parallel and stuck to it. See *A Treatise of Human Nature*, ed. L. A. Selby-Bigge, Clarendon Press, Oxford, 1888, pp. 589-590.

The advent of this new desire halts my activity and has the effect of placing me in a passively reflexive mode of consciousness. In this state of mind, the alternative possibilities presented by the new desire display their advantages and disadvantages and through them I become aware of the ramifications of pursuing this new alternative. Now because of the detached 'spectator' nature of this perspective, the options I now confront are presented to me as if they were advocated by individuals distinct from myself.[10] And my reaction to these requests, i.e. how I feel about the options presented, seems to me to be a disinterested reaction because of the detached nature of the mode of consciousness in which this reaction manifests itself. The 'decision' my reaction indicates presents itself as the one which *anyone* who considered the options would pursue. This gives the decision a feeling of universality (*any* disinterested observer would feel the same way). As a consequence the decision seems to be objectively valid—'right', if you will—because of the passivity of the reflexive state from which it emerges. The 'neutrality' of this state of mind rules out any sense of personal bias which might otherwise be regarded as tainting a judgment based on a subjective element such as a feeling (a reaction).

It is in this way, then, that the passively reflexive mode of consciousness—the judgmental mode we could call it—naturally generates what come to be regarded as *considered* judgments. It is true that these judgments are not strictly speaking rational in character, because a choice between the alternatives presented cannot be made on solely rational grounds according to some rule which Reason, for example, might provide out of its own resources. However this is what we would expect within the realm of the permissible. Reason's rules delineate this realm only in terms of the practical consistency of the maxims under examination. Where two maxims are both approved by Reason, it must be up to some other capacity—judgment—to choose between the permitted options. Our point is that these judgments are regarded as considered judgments because they emanate from the passive reflexive state. The phenomenology of this perspective guarantees that the feelings/decisions which emerge have the right objective 'tone' to them. It is on this factor that the *prima facie* case for the objectivity of judgments based on feelings of this sort rests.

Kant would probably have made no objection to the employment of

---

[10] This is why the tendency to personify the faculties is a natural thing to do when we find ourselves in the passively reflexive mode of consciousness.

our capacity to make judgments in terms of feelings, when it is permitted options we are choosing between. He has no interest in the mechanism whereby we 'decide' between such options since such decisions cannot be regarded as rational. So we might imagine Kant saying—or at least allowing—that it is only when the decision is not a moral one that feelings can play any role. As far as moral decisions are concerned however, he will not move from his view that feelings—as contingent—are not to be trusted. Kant would say that we cannot rely on *judgmental feelings,* as we may style them, when a moral decision is to be made.

In opposition to Kant, we now want to show that the capacity to make judgments based on feelings is the dominant mechanism governing all activities which involve a choice, including moral decision-making. The argument runs as follows.

In the role of disinterested spectator, a role inherent in the phenomenology of passively reflexive states of consciousness, we can discover afresh how we actually feel about engaging in alternative courses of action. Thus, for example, while all was going well and we were concentrating on our task, a particular balance of feelings was motivating us to behave in a particular way. When fresh alternatives present themselves, our capacity to reflect permits us to come to a new balance of feelings. This process of reflection[11] presents itself as a natural way of coming to a decision which will lead us back to action.

We now wish to argue that there is evidence to show that this natural process, through which decisions are made and actions follow, forms an intrusive background to our attempts to behave morally through acts of free will. As such it constitutes a fundamental obstacle to the effectiveness of the pure decision-making device (the act of free will) which Reason must appeal to after it has determined what course of action would be practically valid. (And as we shall see[12] it can also account for what Kant calls the problem of subreption.)

Now the idea that decisions are actively made by us and the idea that our decisions are no more than functions of the way we feel are both reflections of the ambiguous idea we have of ourselves as decision-makers. Thus we can speak of decision-making in both the active and the passive voice. I can say, with equal grammatical probity: 'I have made up my mind about this matter' and, 'My mind is made up about this matter'.

Do I then actively make up my mind or do I find that my mind is

---

[11] Such reflection is not a synonym for reasoning. Reflection is a turning back, a review of our proceedings. It is a mental process, but not one whose results I can determine.

[12] See pp. 54 *ff.*, below.

made up? (That these two options exhaust the possibilities open to us when we try to characterize decision-making is, we believe, a mistake. There is also the possibility that agents—as finite—are neither completely passive nor completely active when they make decisions. What this conception of agency amounts to will be explained in Chapter Five.)

Consider a person with Kantian predilections, one who thinks that decisions are actively made and, indeed, must be actively made if we are to have any dignity as human beings and not simply be subject to natural necessity. When such a person is passively reflexive, listening to the debate between Desire and Reason, and when this debate is naturally concluded through the generation of a certain balance of feelings, there is room for confusion. For such people, these naturally arising judgmental feelings cannot be regarded as constitutive of their decision as to what they are to do, simply because they have not *chosen* to feel this way about the matter. They must then—in order to actively make a decision—assume an active role in the matter. However the difficulty in doing this is that to be an active 'decider' it is necessary to employ some deliberate means—some procedure—for deciding. A person cannot just *decide* (i.e. decide randomly) and still maintain a sense of his or her dignity as a free being.

Now the only active method of deciding which we know how to employ is reasoning hypothetically. This is the process whereby I think about the simplest (most efficient, least expensive, etc.) way to achieve some end which I desire. (I know *how* to do this because I have learned how to do it through past experience. It is a skill which I have acquired.) However, the situation facing our active decision-maker is not one of choosing the best means to a given end, but rather what is to be the end: to do as one ought or as one desires?

It would seem then that this person, convinced that an active decision as to what end to pursue is necessary, will simply be going around in circles if it is thought that this decision can be actively made through reasoning. Hypothetical reasoning is not applicable and that categorical reasoning which serves to determine what this person ought to do has already been engaged in: the practical options open to human reason are exhausted. The fact must therefore be faced that the decision as to what to do must be taken without reference to further reasoning. So, can a person actively decide to behave in accordance with (or in opposition to) the Categorical Imperative? Kant would say that we can do so in virtue of our freedom and he freely admits that how we exercise our freedom is, at bottom, a mystery. However, if we want to resist the pull of this mystery and not treat the whole matter as inscrutable and therefore not open to explanation, it would seem that what we decide to do must depend on whether or not we have developed a feeling for the moral option: whether—as it happens—it matters to us that we be exclusively rational in our behaviour.[13]

Now if such a development has occurred, we will act in accordance with it and we will then seem to have acted in accordance with the dictates of Reason. However, if this happens, this action on our part will seem to us to have been unconstrained: it will not seem to us that we have acted from a sense of obligation, but rather that we have acted naturally (i.e. in accordance with our feelings). With this situation in mind Kant is quick to point out that there is an important difference between acting merely in accordance with duty—producing actions which have legality—and acting *out* of duty—producing actions which have a moral value.[14] Within the moral form of life we must have a sense of having acted freely in order to fulfill an obligation where this involves a sense of constraint (a sense of making a deliberate effort to align one's behaviour with the sense of obligation that one feels). Under these circumstances the problem can arise, as we have just seen, of being in a state of mind in which one's judgmental feelings happen to accord with Reason's dictates and thus finding oneself free of any sense of constraint (of being obliged) as one acts morally.

However if moral value is to be created in such cases, the Kantian must insist that people actively identify with Reason: that they 'mentally affirm' their allegiance to it as they act in order to 'discount' the natural motivational role which their judgmental feelings are playing in their moral behaviour. This active identification with Reason ('Doing one's duty solely out of the thought of duty') is the crucial element which must be present in a moral as opposed to a legal action. If we do not actively identify with Reason (by freely incorporating its laws into our subjective

---

[13] It is at this point that Kant introduces the notion of respect, an "intellectual emotion" generated by the awesome consistency with which categorical reasoning indicates our duty without fear or favour. However, respect is only an incentive to doing our duty, i.e. it does not actually cause us to act. The freedom of the will, and with it our dignity, would be impugned if respect could cause us to act in accordance with the imperative categorical reasoning presents us with. Within the moral form of life, which Kant has defined, respect cannot be a feeling which motivates us the way judgmental feelings do. For a further examination of respect for the moral law, see p. 108 below.

[14] See *CPrR*, p. 180, A 126-127.

maxim[15]) we will not be aware that we have done anything other than act in accordance with our nature as creatures who are motivated by their feelings. So the moral form of life requires that we acknowledge the primacy of Reason's demands. But how did we ever get into this position of having something demanded of us by our rational *persona* (an aspect of ourselves) and yet not necessarily obeying this demand?

The source of the problem is the lengths to which the personification process is taken in the Kantian exposition of morality. When Reason is personified and set up as a categorical authority opposed to Desire, it comes to be seen as something external to us (Reason with a capital 'R'), someone else who gives us orders. However, to have effective (i.e. motivational) authority over us, it cannot be seen as totally external in this way. There must be something of us in it[16] or, alternatively, something in it for us (in terms of some species of happiness which we may expect if we behave as Reason dictates) if the notion of our *deliberately* choosing the moral option is not to simply lapse into mystery.

Now as we have seen, on the naturalistic account of human conduct, what we actually do is a function of our feelings and we simply cannot act unless the feelings that motivate action are present. However, for Kant, this account is unacceptable. Feelings can have no such pre-eminence as the fundamental source of motivation when it is moral behaviour with which we are concerned. Feelings (judgmental or otherwise) are considered by Kant to be mere inclinations which can and must be disregarded by free agents aware of their inherent dignity. An individual's inclinations and preferences cannot be regarded as having any moral authority and, indeed, it must be possible to overcome such feelings by a free act of our will if morality is to be a possibility. Since morality cannot derive from the natural motivational authority of our judgmental feelings, it seems then that an independent source of moral authority must somehow be established. The question is: on what basis will the establishment of this authority rest?

Now we are well aware of the fact that, so far as Kant is concerned, the only active means we have of deciding whether something is right or wrong is *via* the Categorical Imperative. This active process of reasoning determines the realm of what is morally wrong. From this analytic point of view it is the practical inconsistency of an action (the

---

[15] See *RWL*, p. 19, A 10 B 12.

[16] i.e., it must appeal to our ontological instinct to be true to ourselves by presenting itself as our true (and therefore better) self and thus as the source of that dignity which only ontological fidelity can bring about.

analytic point of view it is the practical inconsistency of an action (the self-destructiveness of the practice in question when universally followed) that marks it as morally wrong. Therefore the 'trick', if you will, of establishing the authority of the voice of Reason (as the arbiter of the worth of our conduct) must turn on the acceptance of the equation between 'practically inconsistent' and 'morally wrong', an equation which effectively creates the belief that it matters—supremely—that one should not do things which are practically inconsistent.

Now, how can we come to recognize that it matters supremely whether we act only on maxims which categorical reasoning has declared to be practically consistent? Upon what basis are we to come to acknowledge an overriding (moral) obligation on our part to behave as the Categorical Imperative dictates?

The answer, for Kant, lies in the fact that unless we accept this obligation to be consistent (i.e. to lead a life governed by principles which, when followed, produce practically valid behaviour) we must settle for a life determined by those contingent factors which activate our desires. The spectre of this heteronomous form of life is the force underlying Kant's constant harping on the fact that what is at stake in morality is our dignity as human beings. We cannot be dignified in so far as we conduct ourselves according to the contingent whims of Desire. People must direct their own conduct (i.e. be autonomous) in order to maintain their dignity.

So we can understand why, on the Kantian approach, we feel obliged to follow Reason. It is because on this approach there is no other option if we are to maintain our dignity. If we do not follow Reason we cease to use that faculty in us which can determine lines of conduct autonomously, i.e. through the utilization of its own inherent capacity to distinguish consistent from inconsistent ways of behaving. If we cease to be rational in this sense, we abandon the sole capacity we have for conducting our affairs with dignity, a state of being which requires us to direct our affairs according to rules involving an internal 'guarantee' of their probity.[17]

However, the authority with which we have invested categorical reasoning (based on our recognition of its capacity to provide us with the rules upon which a dignified way of life may be founded) is not sufficient to make us automatically follow its dictates. And this is exactly what we would expect: no influence can be allowed to *determine* a free decision on pain of destroying the moral value of that decision. However this

---

[17] Consistent behaviour is correct behaviour and constitutes the *right* way to behave, the way which has positive moral value.

means that we are back where we started from. It will turn out that, whether or not we act in accordance with the dictates of Reason, our capacity so to act can only appear to us to be a function of whether we are (or are not) in tune (in terms of our judgmental feelings) with the dictates of Reason— unless, of course, we are willing to succumb to the mystery of free will and blithely disregard the motivational force of our feelings as an irrelevant factor in our behaviour.

Furthermore, when we feel in tune with them, the truth is that we feel a sense of modesty with respect to our own 'virtue' since we feel that this is just the way we naturally would have acted: we felt that way and therefore we acted that way.[18] In the same way, if our feelings are at odds with our a priori deliberations as to what we ought to do, then we will feel the same sense of modesty when we act in 'defiance' of these deliberations: it was because we felt this way that we did what we did. Although we must acknowledge these rational deliberations as having authority over us (in that we have so invested them when we acknowledge that they are the only guide to a dignified life) our sense of obligation (which derived from this investiture) may not be strong enough to overcome our feelings. We may not—on a given occasion—be that concerned about living a dignified life. Everything depends on how we feel at the time.

Let us remind ourselves at this point why it is that judgmental feelings have this authority and are able to resist the authority which we invest in Reason when we acknowledge the moral form of life. Judgmental feelings arise from passively reflexive states of consciousness and the point of passively reflecting is to consider the options open to us and, by so doing, to discover how we feel about pursuing them. On the basis of such considerations, a judgment concerning the viability of the options in question is generated. The judgmental feelings which constitute this judgment have, like Reason's computation of where our duty lies, a disinterested and therefore authoritative character. However if such disinterested feelings are not recognized as being an authoritative source of motivation—on the grounds that their status as feelings renders them contingent and therefore unreliable (uncertain) —we thereby give up our natural capacity to arrive at authoritative decisions.

How then does Kant imagine that the natural authority of these

---

[18] Thus I do not feel morally proud of telling the truth under ordinary circumstances. My judgment (my feeling concerning what would be the best thing to do, in terms of its viability) backs up the *a priori* sanction against lying, presumably because telling the truth has been, in the past, generally advantageous to me.

feelings can be disregarded? We want now to suggest that his belief that judgmental feelings can be disregarded stems from the fact that, in the process of becoming reflexively aware of our feelings, the natural authority inherent in the disinterested character of our judgmental feelings cannot be retained. From this passive standpoint feelings can be distanced and, as such, can lose their authority. As distanced such feelings can come to be seen as simply occurrent phenomena and lose the character of authoritative sources by which our behaviour should be guided.

Now there is no doubt that such a sequence is a phenomenological possibility. In the passively reflexive mode of consciousness we always have the option of observing our feelings from a third-person perspective and thus of freeing ourselves from their motivational authority over us. However, the passively reflexive mode of consciousness is only, as it were, a provisional mode of consciousness for an agent. It provides the pause for reflection that allows the agent to *act* instead of simply *re-*acting to circumstances.

However, because we must act eventually, the passively reflexive mode inevitably reverts to an active mode of consciousness. As agents we must become motivated if we are to act. Usually this happens naturally, simply because we naturally identify with our judgmental feelings—they constitute the way *we*[19] feel—and hence constitute our natural motives when we act in the light of our reflections on the options facing us.

On this model of the passively reflexive mode of consciousness the pause for reflection can provide a phenomenological locus—'a place to stand'—from which the agent can be thought of as acting freely, i.e. without reference to those natural motives which—as distanced—can be ignored. So much then for the phenomenological venue which allows for the possibility of an act of free will.

The question remains as to whether any such acts ever occur. In other words, when we act, do we always, in fact, revert to an active mode of consciousness in which our conduct is a function of our motives (our judgmental feelings) or do we, in fact, sometimes act purely through the medium of free acts of will? Can we sometimes act autonomously? Kant recognized this problem; he admits that we can never know whether we have successfully avoided being motivated by such feelings (or indeed any contingent motive) when we act in accordance with Reason's dictates. We can never know whether we have not in fact been subject to a 'subreption'. As Kant puts it:

there is always here an occasion for a subreption (*vitium subretionis*) and,

---

[19] See pp. 70 *ff.*, below, on this special use of *'we'*.

as it were, for an optical illusion in the self-consciousness of what one does in contradistinction to what one feels, which even the most experienced person cannot entirely avoid. The moral disposition is necessarily connected with a consciousness of the determination of the will directly by a law. Now the consciousness of a determination of the faculty of desire[20] is always a ground for satisfaction in the resulting action; but this pleasure, this satisfaction with one's self [*as having followed what one's judgmental feelings indicate as the viable course of action for anyone in our situation*], is not the determining ground of the action [*when we will morally*]; on the contrary [*in so far as we are to be said to achieve moral self-contentment through our willing*], the determination of the will directly by reason alone is the ground of the feeling of pleasure, and this remains a pure practical determination of the faculty of desire [*our capacity to act*], not a sensuous one.[21] Since this [*rational*] determination produces the same inward effect, i.e., an impulse to activity, as does a feeling of agreeableness which is expected from the desired action [the one we are prompted toward by our judgmental feelings], we see that what we ourselves do may easily be looked upon as something which we merely passively feel,[22] the moral motive being held to be a sensuous impulse... (CPrR, pp. 220-221, A 209 -210)

According to this passage it is quite clear that, from an introspective point of view, we can never confirm—with certainty—whether or not the superimposed moral form of causality (free will) has actually overridden the natural causality of our feelings. Therefore Kant can only insist that the distinction is real, noting that

It is a very sublime thing in human nature to be determined to actions directly by a pure law of reason, and even the illusion wherein the subjective element of this intellectual determinability of the will is held to be sensuous and an effect of a particular sensuous feeling (an 'intellectual

---

[20] Kant would regard judgmental feelings as desires since such feelings motivate us in terms of the happiness we will experience if we follow them. (In fact our judgmental feelings result, when followed, in a sense of well-being, an ontological value which is neither happiness nor moral self-contentment. It is the value we discover when we trust ourselves, when we trust our judgmental feelings as constituting our self's core.)

[21] Judgmental feelings would be sensuous in Kant's view.

[22] It is the term 'merely' which we object to, since on our analysis of the way in which judgmental feelings are generated, their 'passivity' is the source of their disinterestedness and thus of their authority for us. There is nothing 'mere' about them.

feeling' being self-contradictory) partakes of this sublimity. (*CPrR*, p. 221, A 210)

Kant cannot conceive of the possibility that Reason cannot be practical, therefore there simply must be occasions on which it is Reason's law which motivates us and occasions on which it is 'merely' our feelings. Indeed the thing is so sublime that even the illusion we suffer, confusing sensuous and rational motivation, is itself to be wondered at.

So, in the end, we confront the spectacle of our own epistemic weakness with reference to behaving morally. We see that we can never know with certainty whether we have acted solely out of respect for the moral law. We are aware that we may, in fact, always be acting in accordance with our judgmental feelings. And this poses a serious problem since such feelings have no moral status. Thus the actual role of these feelings in our behaviour remains as a persistent problem for the Kantian human agent, who can only deal with the problem *via* the doctrine of subreption, *via* the fact that we can never, in the nature of the case, know whether we have willed solely out of the thought of duty or not. The possibility that moral behaviour may occur is left open, but only as a consequence of the fact that Kant's theory of moral value—as an autonomously created value—*requires* the existence of such a theoretically distinctive, indeed unique, mode of causality. We can have no unimpeachable introspective evidence of the reality of moral behaviour as an an actual form of life.

Why then do we persist in acknowledging this form of life? Is there in fact no alternative? We believe there is and a further examination of the grounds for the Kantian agent's persistent belief in the moral form of life will provide the basis for demonstrating the adequacy of this alternative understanding of moral decision-making.

III

In this chapter we have, thus far, pointed out that the passively reflexive mode of consciousness exhibits a phenomenology which allows for the possibility of moral behaviour. However, the passively reflexive mode of consciousness was also seen to have a judgmental capacity built into its operation which served as the foundation of a natural means of coming to decisions. And we have indicated the way in which moral decision-making was able to superimpose itself onto this natural process of deciding. In essence it is able to do this by exploiting the third person, or 'spectator', perspective which is one element of the passively reflexive mode of consciousness. On our interpretation, by concentrating on this 'neutral observer' element, the Kantian agent was able to posit a phenomenological locus in which its freedom as an agent might be exercised—untainted by any dispositional influence.

The key factor in keeping the moral method of decision-making in the ascendant is the move whereby the Kantian agent carefully downgrades its judgmental feelings to the status of inclinations. This is accomplished by emphasizing the neutrality which can be attained when we adopt a passively reflexive standpoint. From this point of view the spectator self is able to distance its feelings and thus regard them, for the moment, as 'mere feelings' (feelings which are not a part of the central make-up of the self which notes their presence). It can therefore also regard itself as not under the influence of these natural motives when it makes a decision. However this neutral perspective can only be maintained with great effort. For it is in fact natural for such spectators to experience judgmental feelings *as their own* and (when making decisions) to experience them altering and coming to rest in a motivational set which makes the person who feels them no longer a mere spectator but an actor. These feelings remain as an intrusion upon any attempt to act freely in the Kantian fashion.

With this in mind, how does the Kantian agent come to maintain its pure spectator perspective and downgrade the natural motivational significance of judgmental feelings? More to the point, why do agents persist in their endeavours to disregard the natural authority of their judgmental feelings? Only it would seem, through a conception of moral conduct which necessitates the maintenance of this perspective as a condition of the very possibility of a free exercise of the will and therefore of morally valuable conduct. This conception is rooted in the idea that there is a kind of human action for which responsibility can be imputed solely to the agent concerned, viz. moral action stemming from the free exercise of the will. A free exercise of the will is the absolute foundation of the moral form of life. The notion that such a free exercise of the will must be the origin of moral behaviour turns on the further notion that a moral act is one over which the agent has *complete* control. To maintain this sort of control, the agent who acts must be isolated from any dispositional factors which could sully the absolute freedom of action which grounds the moral value of its choices. The only way to achieve this is to isolate the locus of the free act which creates moral values from any factors which could explain why any particular decision took the direction that it did. This is because any successful explanation in terms of natural causality would explain away the possibility of imputing this conduct solely to the agent and, with it, the notion of any moral value attaching to this conduct. The creation of moral value through a free act of choice must then appear as a break with natural behaviour, a break which individual people make *solely on their own initiative*.

Furthermore, the structure of the passively reflexive mode of consciousness ensures that, in principle, the agent *can* be neutral. Passive reflection provides the phenomenological possibility for the 'spectator' perspective which serves to explain how an agent can (phenomenologically) be in a position to distance itself from its judgmental feelings. It does not, of course, explain how the agent exercises its freedom of choice from this neutral position. However, by isolating the agent in this spectator perspective, it professes to show that, whatever the agent does do, it need not be attributed to dispositions brought about by the capacity to experience judgmental feelings. These feelings can always be distanced from the agent, thus allowing a gap for free choice.[23]

Now because we do actually escape from the motivational stalemate created when Desire's wants conflict with Reason's dictates, free choice must somehow bridge this gap. Natural causality can play no part in accounting for this free activity so long as we maintain a conception of ourselves as beings which can actually exercise their agency without reference to external causal factors. So the causality of freedom[24] must be brought in to underwrite the possibility of human agency being exercised as the moral form of life demands.

It is a part of our thesis that it is a mistake to adopt this view of agency as free—in this absolute sense—even though it is a phenomenological possibility. The mistake lies in not recognizing that our feelings are an inalienable part of ourselves and that, therefore, isolating them necessarily leads to those psychological problems which arise when we do not acknowledge the natural authority of our judgmental feelings. However if we do acknowledge the authority of our feelings, do

---

[23] This is an argument which, on the phenomenological level, mirrors Kant's own metaphysical argument known as the 'Two Standpoints' argument by which he critically resolves Antinomies. See CPrR, pp. 218 *ff.*, A 205 *ff.*, e.g. "When we see ourselves obliged to seek at such a distance—namely, in the context of an intelligible world—the possibility of the highest good... " (p. 219, A 207).

[24] *CPR*, p. 464, A 532 B 560.

we throw away all chance of realizing that unique value which is the product of the moral form of life? We do in a way, but to measure our loss we must again consider the basis of the value which we naturally attach to the kind of decision-making which is based on judgmental feelings.

Judgmental feelings are the product of reflection. Reflection, because of its passivity, allows our feelings to settle in a natural way, gradually coalescing into a new motivational set as fresh experiences are integrated with what we already know. The motivational strength of this alternative way of coming to decisions lies in the fact that people cannot externalize or project or personify the process of discovering how they feel. Thus when I propose to see how I feel about something, I cannot do anything to work out how I am going to feel about it other than laying out the ramifications of the alternatives as I understand them and saying to myself (as to a child) 'Now which do I really prefer, this, or this?' Once the alternatives are laid out, I have done all that I can to determine my feelings and I must then simply see (find out, discover) how I actually feel. The crucial aspect of this practice is that I cannot think of the feelings which emerge as 'merely' mine, that is, open to alienation through thinking of them as 'my' feelings as if I who note them were different from I who experience them.

That we *can* alienate them is, as we have seen, Kant's view and we have seen that the phenomenology of the passively reflexive mode of consciousness allows for such a view. Kant then regards such judgmental feelings as having only a contingent association with us and, as contingent, they can have no status as authoritative guides to conduct. Kant takes this view because he believes that morality must not be a function of anything that changes with experience or that varies with circumstances. Naturally occurring dispositions (the new motivational sets constituted by judgmental feelings) are classified by Kant as inclinations since they are contingent (they could have been other than they are) and are therefore considered irrelevant in the moral field once it is recognized that moral judgments must be regarded as certain. In other words, despite the *disinterested* character of those feelings which occur when we passively reflect on a problem (to see how we really feel about it) these feelings are equated by Kant with inclinations, the vehicles for the variable *interest* we have in things around us.

This is the central point of our dispute with Kant. In our view, this reduction of judgmental feelings to the status of inclinations is not legitimate. What separates these two sorts of emotions is the fact that judgmental feelings are the responses that result from our consideration of various alternatives (they are the end results of periods of passive reflection), whereas inclinations are simply unreflective reactions to immediate stimuli. Thus we do not simply react to the alternatives before us when they are presented in states of reflexive consciousness. Rather we observe that we feel uneasy,[25] say, about doing x as opposed to y: we don't feel 'right' about it, where 'right' indicates a concern not confined to the short term prospect of doing x, but instead indicates a concern for the *viability* of the chosen course of action. Such a feeling amounts to an impersonal concern with our capacity to live with behaviour of this sort. By contrast, inclinations *per se* do not have a right or wrong, easy or uneasy character to them. They bear no witness to the viability of the conduct they urge upon us. What is different about judgmental feelings is that they are bound up with the process of passive reflection. It is the 'processed' character of such considerations which renders the resultant judgmental feelings authoritative in relationship to our projected behaviour. In so far as reflection allows us to stand back from our immediate inclinations and to consider how we actually feel about the behaviour which they incline us towards, it is disinterested and impersonal. When we reflect, we view our prospective actions or plans as if from a point of view that is independent of ourselves (insofar as we identify ourselves with our immediate inclinations). We thus view them from a universal perspective, from the viewpoint of any reflective human being in the same situation.

It is for this reason that the *subjective* effect of this passively reflexive mode of consciousness, viz. our judgmental feelings, can provide a procedure for judging the viability of our future conduct which is just as disinterested, impersonal and reliable as any judgment handed down by Reason. Admittedly, judgmental feelings will change over time and vary with circumstances, but this is just what makes them so trustworthy as guides to future conduct. They can be used to indicate very precisely where the well-being of ourselves and those around us lies in an unending variety of situations. They may not be certain in the absolute sense of being set or preordained through *a priori* reasoning and thus good for any agent in any situation but they can be depended on to inform us of the viability of a proposed action in the light of the experience we have acquired in the past. Judgmental feelings are therefore a suitably

---

[25] Hume's term 'uneasiness' describes the tone of a negative judgmental feelings perfectly. See *A Treatise of Human Nature*, ed. L. A. Selby-Bigge, Clarendon Press, Oxford, 1888, p. 475 & p. 589.

means of directing our lives.[26]

Due to our natural identification with them they move us to act: they are enabling. What judgmental feelings chart out is not the area charted out by moral judgments, viz. those acts which are categorized as permitted or forbidden. Rather they chart out the behaviour one can live with as opposed to behaviour which causes one to feel uneasy. And we maintain that it is simply a natural fact that no one can live uneasily for very long (in opposition to their judgmental feelings) without suffering mental distortions of one sort or another. For how, after all, save through such distortions, could one protect oneself from those reflexive states of consciousness in which uneasiness lurks, ever ready to disturb our sense of well-being and self-contentment whenever our actions run counter to our judgmental feelings. It is impossible to distance judgmental feelings from our sense of self for any length of time. They have an inalienable connection with us because they sum up our experience as agents: they constitute the substance of our sense of identity as finite agents with a limited history and give us a sense of what constitutes viable and 'uneasy' behaviour derived from that history.

By comparison it is quite easy to ignore judgments made from a distanced or third-person point of view: for instance, judgments which present themselves as Reason's view of how one ought to behave. Thus it is possible not to care about telling a lie where all one recognizes is the practical invalidity of such a practice. However to ignore first-person judgments—what we have found through reflection that we actually care about—could only be accomplished through some sort of disassociation of one's personality. An excellent example of this consequence is Kant's own case of a man not caring, or at least saying that he will not care, about no one helping him when he needs help.[27] This is a situation in which the Categorical Imperative does not rule out such behaviour on the grounds that it would be practically invalid, but rather on psychological grounds:

Now although it is possible that a universal law of nature according to that maxim could exist, it is nevertheless impossible to will that such a

---

[26] That is, lives led by finite agents with only a limited store of experience on which to base their endeavours.

[27] This is Kant's fourth example in *FMM*: "For a will which resolved this [not to care] would conflict with itself, since instances can often arise in which he would need the love and sympathy of others, and in which he would have robbed himself, by such a law of nature springing from his own will, of all hope of the aid he desires." (p. 82, BA 56)

principle should hold everywhere as a law of nature. (*FMM*, p. 82, AB 56)

Kant is here virtually acknowledging the fact that our freedom to will according to maxims is constrained by our particular nature as feeling creatures (in this case creatures who will, as a matter of fact, hope for love and sympathy from others in times of hardship). He is then, in so many words, recognizing that we have a duty to confine our behaviour to lines of action which will be psychologically viable, which will not be in conflict with our nature as feeling creatures.

We have now seen that judgmental feelings, as a function of passive reflection, are reliable indicators of what line of action is best for us in terms of its viability.[28] Furthermore, because we naturally identify with these feelings they will have a motivational authority that we cannot ignore without putting the natural integrity of our personality at risk. There is then no effective alternative to the motivational power of our judgmental feelings, so far as the experience of our own behaviour can testify.

It is important in all of this to appreciate the status of feelings as constituting *the* way of knowing ourselves in relation to our world as a field of action. Utilizing the neutral spectator standpoint available to us through passive reflection, we may be said to know the world 'objectively', i.e. as a line-up of things presented to a passive spectator-self, things which are related by similarities and differences which reasoning comprehends. However the presence of the self as an involved agent is also an aspect of this mode of consciousness and, from this engaged point of view, we automatically relate these 'objective' things to ourselves: we consider how the world affects us and what we should do in it. Feelings are the pragmatic element in the passively reflexive mode of consciousness because they form a link between neutral, objective views of our situation and our view of the situation as the agents involved. They thus provide us with the only means we have of knowing how things stand between us—*as agents*—and our environment. Thus, from

---

[28] The reliability of the emotions as indicators—here of truth—is captured nicely by R. Pasotti in 'Spinoza: the Metaphysician as Healer' in *Spinoza's Metaphysics*, ed. T. B. Wilbur, Van Gorcum, Assen, 1976, pp. 106-114, e.g. "The emotions act as purveyors of the working order of nature to the adequate mind through the healthy body. These Spinozistic synapses are the most accurate sources of knowledge of the external world. On the other hand, false ideas (their erroneous arrangement) are the signs of emotional-bodily malfunctioning. Their presence too is signified by bodily feelings, sorrow, despair, pain, negativity. Somehow, a false idea hurts, it isn't right. Contrariwise, a true idea feels good. It heightens our bodily powers and perceptions. The emotional joy it produces in us signifies its truth." (p. 113)

the point of view of the reflexive agent, you *are* your feelings, they are what gives your agency substance and direction, which is why acting with regard to your feelings constitutes being true to your self as a being capable of activity. What we will henceforth term *natural* morality is simply a matter of being true to these (judgmental) feelings in acting.[29]

Kantian morality also draws upon this ultimate source of value of being true to one's own nature. In holding up willing in accordance with Reason as its ultimate value, Kantian morality thinks of rational willing as the expression of one's true being. Human beings are both sensible and rational, but it is only the rational half that really matters according to Kant. The sensible (or animal) aspect is just an impediment to the realization of our true nature. However, in the process of seeing the ability to reason (as opposed to our capacity to seek satisfaction) as constitutive of our true nature, reason is personified and immediately presents itself as a dictator-from-without. But Reason in this personified sense is only a partial representation of our nature, and, as personified, makes a demand to take total charge of our behaviour, a demand that inevitably appears to us to be an imposition. Furthermore, nothing that commands externally can have the ontological authority or the conviction of feelings since, while people can break the moral law and escape unscathed, no one can disobey his or her judgmental feelings without suffering the profound unhappiness which comes with being at odds with one's natural self.

With this we bring to a close our discussion of how the passively reflexive mode of consciousness grounds both the form of life we call natural morality and allows for the superimposition of the moral form of life epitomized by Kant. We have argued that the Kantian form of morality does not effectively mask or displace natural morality and that the natural motivational authority of the latter stands in the way of the moral form of life establishing itself as a viable method of determining our behaviour.

However, if we are right and the moral form of life is not a practical way of leading one's life, it is still the case that it continues and will continue to attract attention because of the special character of the value it claims to create. Does natural morality have the power to create a kind of value which may stand as a worthy rival of moral value? In the next chapter we will lay the groundwork for answering this question.

---

[29] Note that, in line with earlier comments (see, e.g., p. 16), 'natural' here does not entail a mechanistic determinism. Our naturalism is *agent-natualism*.

CHAPTER FOUR

GROUNDWORK FOR A TRANSITION TO SPINOZA

We now turn to Spinoza's alternative account of the source of value in human life, an account in which an understanding of the nature of judgmental feelings, rather than attempts to freely exercise the will, takes centre stage as the means of realizing this value. In order to provide the reader with a clear perspective from which to appreciate this alternative, we now wish to set out and connect the various theses of the first three chapters.

Our governing thesis, set out in Chapter One, is related to Kant's need to maintain his view that the moral value of an action in no way rests upon the happiness (the utility value) that the person in question (or anyone else for that matter) may or may not experience as a result of acting as morality demands. According to Kant virtue must be its own reward or there can be no such thing as virtue.

To support this position Kant had to find a way around the problem set by the fact that

> philosophers of both ancient and modern times have been able to find happiness in very just proportion to virtue in *this* life (in the world of sense) or at least have been able to convince themselves of it. (*CPrR*, p. 219, A 208)

This last phrase prepares the way for Kant's later contention that these philosophers mistook themselves when they thought they experienced happiness in just proportion to their virtuous conduct. In fact, what they experienced was 'self-contentment'. Kant explains how the mistake was made:

> Do we not have a word to denote a satisfaction with existence, *an analogue* of happiness which necessarily accompanies the consciousness of virtue, and which does not indicate a gratification, as "happiness" does?

We do, and this word is "self-contentment", which *in its real meaning* refers only to negative satisfaction with existence in which one is conscious of needing nothing. (*CPrR*, p. 221, A 211-212, our italics)

This cannot be called happiness, since it does not depend upon a positive participation of feeling. (*CPrR*, p. 222, A 214, our italics)

Kant's thesis then is that—understood properly—self-contentment is not a species of happiness and virtuous conduct cannot therefore be conceived of as stemming from a desire to gain happiness through acting virtuously, as people might hitherto have thought. As we see it, this careful redefinition of self-contentment—an attempt to purge it of any qualities which might make it inherently attractive to human beings—was a function of Kant's deep conviction that the moral form of life, though not natural (not a result of Nature but of Freedom) is, nevertheless, real. In other words, despite the fact that the moral form of life is orientated towards a value which people could not be said to seek owing to their nature (in the way that they seek food when hungry) yet, as a way of life, it is no 'vain chimera' but a way of behaving, the possibility of which must be defended at all costs. What we have dubbed 'the shadow model of moral causality' was Kant's attempt to make a case, on the basis of our experience, for the existence of a moral form of life as a real (albeit ultimately mysterious) way of acting which human beings are actually capable of pursuing.

Our counter-thesis is, in essence, that while human experience does allow room for Kant's thesis to be put forward intelligibly (with the *proviso* that there is a mystery at its core concerning our freedom) that same experience is subject to a natural interpretation which obviates the need to make reference to a distinctive form of life in order to explain specifically 'moral' aspects of our experience.

As an introduction to this, consider how the dialogue in Chapter Two would continue if Desire were allowed to persist in its conviction that the claim that moral behaviour creates (*ex nihilo*) a distinctive value is unfounded and that, in fact, moral behaviour is just a special, albeit extra-special, way of securing utility value.

(Desire takes up the issue that has been bothering it throughout its discussion with Conscience:)

Desire: What you are saying is that I must accept that acting on principle is always and absolutely of value, while acting to secure happiness is only incidentally so.

Conscience: Yes, that's right. That is the crux of the matter. All you need to do if you are to acknowledge the moral form of life is to recognize the supreme value of behaving in accordance with those maxims which Reason has shown to be universalizable.

Desire: But why should I value actions just because they are in line with universalizable maxims and are therefore practically valid? Consider, for example the practice of truth-telling. I agree with you that if everyone told lies, the practice of lying would self-destruct. But why does this matter? Surely what matters is the loss of that mutual trust and regard that exists between people in so far as they acknowledge each other to be truth-tellers. And it is the maintenance of this mutual trust which is the real aim of all your moral rules, or so it seems to me. Isn't it the case that this feeling of mutual trust is the *sine qua non* of our happiness? So, yes, truth-telling is vitally important to human beings, but not because Reason has shown *a priori* that the practice of lying is practically invalid. It is the *consequences* of lying that matter, not lying itself.

Conscience: No. The wrongness of telling lies is not a function of its imprudence. I must repeat that it is wrong to tell lies, not because it is disadvantageous, but because it is wrong, period.

Desire: Well then, does it follow that telling the truth has value just because truth-telling is right, period. Consider what would happen if everyone always told the truth. Surely this notion of 'telling the truth' would become meaningless, since there would be no opposite practice, in comparison with which it would be distinguishable. And it follows, *a fortiori*, that truth-telling would cease to be recognizable as a moral practice and cease to have any moral value.

Conscience: Well it's a nice point. People would still be telling the truth all right, but they wouldn't be aware of themselves as doing something right when they followed this practice simply because they wouldn't be aware of the possibility of *not* following this practice.

Desire: So you would concede that the moral value of truth-telling would self-destruct if this practice were universally followed and yet it is certainly not obvious that the utility value of truth-telling would disappear. You would still presumably agree that truth-telling—even when universally practised—is a valuable way to behave. It is valuable because it constitutes the basis of trust between people—call it *communitas*—without which there can be no sense of secure interaction with others and hence no chance for happiness.

Conscience: Certainly.

<u>Desire:</u> Then it seems to follow that the value of *moral* value disappears as soon as the practice that engenders it becomes universal. However, since it retains its utility value, this points to the possibility, indeed, to the likelihood, that the value of moral behaviour always lay in the utility value of the practices it sanctioned. It never lay in their pure rightness (in their being in accordance with practically valid principles) but lay instead in their being a step towards the ideal of preserving *communitas*. It begins to look as if morality exists as a form of life *because* these *communitas*-values are so important (as constituting the *sine qua non* of the possibility[1] of successfully pursuing all other satisfactions) that although they are natural values (species of happiness) they need a special, a moral, sanction to mark their primacy and to ensure their realization. Once we recognize that the rest of life's satisfactions are contingent upon our success in maintaining this background sense of well-being stemming from mutual trust, we can begin to appreciate the real foundation of the categorical force which moral imperatives have. They prohibit those sorts of behaviour which would undermine mutual trust. But in doing so it is not the practical invalidity—the irrationality—of these practices which they warn against (the mere fact that lying wouldn't make any sense if everyone tried to use it to escape from their difficulties). What they warn us against is the fact that immoral practices destroy any possibility of achieving happiness by destroying its basis—*communitas*.

So I would suggest to you that morality in fact exists to provide a special kind of protection for these community values. These values need morality to protect them because, due to their pervasive character (rather like health when you have it) these values tend not to be appreciated when we are in possession of them. Morality then has the appearance of not being practised in order to achieve happiness, because it does not issue in obvious satisfactions. Rather it delivers its rewards in terms of a steady background sense of well-being associated with trusting behaviour.[2] The kind of happiness that attaches to both physical health and peace of mind (born of mutual trust) is, in fact, best recognized in its absence. Without either the reminder (and encouragement) of social mores concerning keeping fit and eating the proper food in the proper amounts, people would easily forget the importance of good health and as a result lose it. Likewise, without the admonitions of morality, people can forget

---

[1] This is perhaps what Kant meant by saying that happiness could not really be enjoyed if one was not worthy of it. Cf. p. 4, above.

[2] In other words, Kant's 'negative satisfaction'.

the importance of maintaining a fundamental trust among themselves.

<u>Conscience:</u> Well I must admit that all my injunctions do concern the categorical importance of maintaining mutual trust. It is these relations between people which form the background of society and I must grant that to be in a state of mutual trust is vital to one's happiness, though perhaps this fact is only clearly appreciated when the trust is lost. That, I suppose, is why my injunctions tend, on the whole, to be negative, since I am constantly warning people about the danger of losing the jewel they possess but whose value is not evident when the conditions for its realization are being maintained. This is why I now insist that my criterion of value—moral rectitude—keep its supremacy. Striving to do what is right, to do one's duty, is the key to maintaining mutual trust. Mutual trust, I agree, is what people want, but if they are to have it its maintenance cannot be their deliberate and leading motive. For that would amount to a kind of deviousness. Morality has to be treated as an end in itself otherwise it won't work. For an agent to ensure its well-being it cannot follow the short-sighted path of prudence. It must treat its supreme concerns as unconditional, as having absolute moral value.

<u>Desire:</u> But how can you hold to this view when you know that absolute moral value is, in the end, the highest good simply because it leads to the supreme utility value—*communitas*? Isn't this deception at the highest level?

What we have here is an attempt to explain away morality by suggesting that moral behaviour derived its special mystique (the view that moral behaviour creates a value that is worth actualizing whatever consequences it may have in terms of human happiness) from the fact that its prudential character—its employment as a means to secure happiness—was masked by its essentially preventative role. That is to say, moral behaviour is designed to avoid the loss of that background happiness which pervades our lives when we trust others and are trusted by them. However this value behind morality, this maintenance of background happiness, is in fact a kind of value that is not appreciated for itself. This is so simply because of its pervasive character when it is actually being maintained through trusting (moral) behaviour. It is not something we take much notice of because it is always there. As a consequence, a desire for this sort of happiness does not normally operate as a motivating factor when—*in the full possession of it*—we perform those moral actions which serve to maintain it in existence. On this view the practice of morality is actually prudential because it prevents us from taking a short-sighted view of the value of that background happiness which depends upon our maintaining trusting relationships. Indeed this value is presented to children as a state worth pursuing for the happiness it will bring, a fact they readily appreciate because of their being more apt to lose it as immediate desires tempt them to betray the trust of others and thus bring them to the sharp distress of losing that trust. The rules for the maintenance of mutual trust are thus often presented to children as prudential rules while being taught as *moral* precepts.

As adults, we may actually regard these prudential rules as being principles with universal practical validity and thus as deserving of moral regard on Kantian grounds. However the injunctions to follow them can never be shorn of their prudential roots. Thus to insist that one keep one's promises on moral grounds alone (simply because it is right to do so) is to forget, in a quite remarkable fashion, the unhappiness which invariably (so far as human experience will attest) attends those who forget this basic ground-rule of social life. This argument then is no more than a version of the familiar claim that morality is, at bottom, a form of prudence.

We have supported this view in Chapter Three where an explanation is given of how a particular mode of consciousness, the passive reflexive mode, could serve as a basis for both a natural method of decision-making (based on judgmental feelings aimed at securing our happiness) and a moral method of decision-making (based on free choice and aimed at creating moral value). We showed that the superimposition of the moral method on the natural method created a situation in which no certain judgment could be made by the agent as to whether, on a given occasion, it acted naturally or morally. This argument was secured through reference to Kant's own discussion of the phenomenon of subreption.

In order to develop further this 'naturalistic' explanation of morality we must now turn to an examination of the nature of the being behind it all—the human agent who experiences this debate between Desire and Conscience (Reason's categorical *persona*). We will endeavour to demonstrate that a Spinozistic understanding of human agency, in contradistinction to the Kantian view, will allow for a prudential rationale to underpin morality without damaging the strength and majesty of the values and experiences associated with the distinctively *moral* form of life.

CHAPTER FIVE

SPINOZA'S ACCOUNT OF HUMAN AGENCY

Spinoza's conception of human agency[1] is difficult to grasp because he does not think of agency either as free or as determined, but instead as more or less free/determined. The difficulty lies in understanding what *'more or less* free/determined' can mean? There is no obvious logical room between the concepts of 'free' and 'determined' so how does Spinoza stake out this middle ground?

What this difficulty actually amounts to can perhaps be best illustrated by considering our knowledge of our agency as exemplified in our capacity for speech.[2] If I ask myself how I am able to speak, I am forced eventually to the conclusion that I do not know how I do it, that somehow I just am able to do it.[3] My capacity for speech (my agency in this regard) is exercised spontaneously and yet the use of this term must not be taken to imply that the speaking is happening on its own and that I am no more than a mere spectator of this speechifying. On the contrary, *I* do it. I am in control (and something is wrong if I am not). I can stop doing it or do something else if I choose. But now what about this 'choosing'? Is this a capacity under my control? I am inclined to claim immediately that of course I am in control of what I choose to do in that I can choose to do otherwise if I want to. Yet here, in the same breath, I am both assuming that I control my own agency and

---

[1] Although we shall be using Spinoza's conception of human agency to guide our discussion of this topic, we do not, for the present purposes, need to set it in the context of his wider philosophical views. His conception of human agency is in fact thoroughly grounded in his metaphysics but the scope of this study does not permit us to delve into this area of his work. For the reader who is interested in exploring this topic we recommend H. F. Hallett's *Benedict de Spinoza: The Elements of his Philosophy* (Athlone Press, London, 1957).

[2] For Spinoza's discussion of our experience of ourselves as agents with a capacity for speech, See *Ethics*, pp. 134-5, III Proposition II Note.

[3] Cf. e.g. Arthur C. Danto, *Analtical Philosophy of Action*, Cambridge University Press, Cambridge, 1973, Chapter 2 'Basic Actions and Basic Cognitions', especially p. 30.

acknowledging—in the very fact that I use the term 'if' (in 'if I want to')—the implication that my control over my choice will be contingent upon some further factor, viz. whether I in fact want to do x rather than y. And again I face the same quandary. Does it make sense to say that the exercise of my agency is subject to certain contingent facts about what I want when, after all, surely it is *I* who do the wanting?

This retreat to an italicized 'I' signifies my apparent inability to characterize my agency in a satisfactory fashion. (Here the use of the term 'satisfactory' implies that unless I can characterize my agency either as free or as determined then I had better keep trying since it must be characterizable under one of these exhaustive alternatives, there being nothing in between.) It constitutes a declaration that, in this case, where I am trying to understand the nature of my agency, I lack the means to explain clearly my understanding of my status of an agent. It marks the point at which I am depending upon my reader to grasp intuitively what I am trying to convey about my being as an agent.

This 'retreat to italics' is a common (though unremarked) phenomenon and deserves to be properly categorized: we propose to call it an 'emphatic metaphor'. The italicized 'I' is metaphorical in that it is a rhetorical device which seeks to convey an inexpressible something about the phenomenon under examination. It is emphatic in that it accomplishes this task simply by 'bearing down' upon the name of the phenomenon in question, thereby directing the reader's attention to his or her own intuition[4] of this phenomenon which, it is presumed, matches that of the person using the emphatic metaphor.

Emphatic metaphors are well established in use as our linguistic means of conveying our intuitive knowledge of various phenomena including the understanding of our agency. In using such locutions we feel confident that others know what we mean by them as well as we do and we do this in spite of the fact that our reliance on mere emphasis to get across to others the apparently inexpressible quality of our intuition might seem to cast a shadow over our confidence and indeed to amount to an admission that we are, in reality, unable to make our intuitions intelligible. All we can do, it seems, is 'point' emphatically in the direction of the phenomenon in question. However it would be a mistake

---

[4] Kant was convinced that such attempts to know ourselves in this intuitive fashion were ruled out by the constitution of our understanding i.e. in order to know anything it was necessary to bring an intuition under a concept. The retreat to an emphatic metaphor in the case before us may be said to prove his point. See CPR, pp. 167-169 B 155-159; Ethics, IV, Prop. 35.

to suppose that emphatic metaphors are a sign of a total failure to communicate our intuitions. In fact, these emphatic metaphors are quite legitimate devices whose particular role in the language is to give expression to our most fundamental experiences, including our understanding of the unique relationship we have with our own powers as agents.

Returning now to the point at issue: the quandary which arises when we try to characterize our sense of being agents centres on a conflict between our sense of being in control of what we do and an appreciation of the contingencies which seem to govern the existence of those motives which must be posited in order to explain why we do what we do. Of course I can do whatever I want to do, but is this 'wanting' something that I do in the sense of something I can control? In answering this question we feel like saying something like this: sometimes I do motivate myself— more or less consciously—and sometimes I do not, but even when I do not, I do not feel like I am being compelled by the emotions that motivate me. My motives are still mine, whether it seems to me that I consciously bring them into being or whether they simply seem to occur as an expression of *my* character. Some of my motives are more mine than others. My sense of myself as an agent is my sense of possessing a mitigated capacity to motivate myself. Thus when I use an emphatic metaphor in common speech ('Surely it is *I* who do the wanting.') what I am trying to convey is this sense of mitigation with respect to my control over my motives and hence of my agency.

Common experience reveals the status of our agency as a mitigated capacity to control what motivates our behaviour. Building on this foundation we can begin, following Spinoza, to draw out a number of implications of this fact in our assessment of the human condition. This enterprise is the principal task of Spinoza's *Ethics*, a work which aims to explain how a finite being—a being whose power as an agent is fundamentally mitigated—should conduct its life once it comes to understand the nature of its own agency.

First Implication

What follows then from the fact that our agency is mitigated, i.e. from the fact that we are *finite* agents? The first implication is that we are never either completely in control or completely out of control, never entirely active or entirely passive in the exercise of our agency. Whatever we do, we are always *more or less* subject to agencies beyond our control which either cooperate with or tend to frustrate our endeavours. However, at the same time, whatever happens to us is always more or less a consequence of the active exercise of our agency. Because we are finite (= limited), we can never act without some outside influence playing a part in what we do. By the same token, we can never be fully controlled, fully determined by other agencies without losing our essential nature as agents. We can conclude from this that the possibilities open to us in exercising our agency will all involve interaction with other agents.

Second Implication

The second implication of understanding agency as mitigated relates to the character of our involvement with other similar agents. For a finite agent, because its endeavours always involve interaction with other agents, the relative success of these endeavours will be a function of the degree to which these endeavours constitute harmonious interactions. A simple illustration of this aspect of our agency is provided by the situation in which two people are sawing a log with a double-handled saw. So long as their endeavour is characterized by reciprocal (harmonious) interaction, it will be a success, subject only to the other 'agent' involved—the log—which may or may not 'cooperate' with the endeavour, may or may not give way easily to the teeth of the saw. (These scare quotes are an acknowledgment that, although from the point of view of Spinoza's metaphysics all finite things are agents, we tend not to feel comfortable speaking of human and non-human agents in the same breath. We tend to think that human agents are the only true agents because of the essential link we feel exists between thought and action, properly so called. Thus animals are regarded as simply behaving when they 'act' because we regard them as incapable of thought and therefore somehow governed in their 'endeavours' by internal drives whose status as 'thoughts' is moot. Again, sticks and stones, considered as agents, are one step lower and 'behave' in strict accordance to the laws of nature which are regarded as determining their 'endeavours' as if they themselves contributed nothing at all to what happens to them. However, in ordinary language, there are no hard and fast rules governing these attributions (or refusals to attribute) agency. An interesting example of this is provided in the case of children: their behaviour is not thought of as completely determined by their upbringing. However we still regard their endeavours as being more or less a function of how they are brought up. This is why we speak of their 'behaviour' (as opposed to their *actions*) and thus indicate with this term that we think of children's actions as being relatively passive, i.e. largely functions of other agents' activities.)

This involvement with other agents (and the necessity that this involvement be *harmonious* if we are to achieve success in our personal endeavours) is not simply a contingent and derivative fact concerning human existence so far as Spinoza is concerned. The Spinozistic human being is not a self-contained unit which happens to be cast among others with whom it must then cooperate for its own benefit. Human endeavour necessarily involves interaction with other agents. It is their status as individuals (beings endeavouring to succeed 'on their own' as it were) which is secondary and derivative, a function of the agent's ignoring the reciprocal character of human action and treating itself as an independent (and self-sufficient) centre of activity. Harmonious interaction between agents is thus not just a desirable (and therefore necessarily optional) extra. It is the only way—according to Spinoza —that agents can express themselves if they are to be true to their nature.

Third Implication

A third implication of mitigated agency rests on the way in which we experience the relative success of our endeavours. The knowledge human agents have that they are succeeding in their endeavours is manifested to them by the fact that they feel more joy (pleasure) the more active their endeavours are. In short, human beings are so constituted that they experience various *affects* (pleasure and pain) to a degree relative to the extent to which their agency is harmoniously engaged. Related to this we find that there is no satisfaction which marks a total end to endeavour. Permanent contentment is not the natural lot of the finite agent because there is always room for improvement so far as the harmony of its activities are concerned. Perfection, then, is a kind of scandal where human activity is involved.

Fourth Implication

The fourth implication of human agency's being finite is related directly to the third. It would seem that, in so far as human beings are inherently dissatisfied (in the sense that they are constantly seeking increased levels of activity in order to experience the joy that accompanies such increments) they will, as a matter of fact, endeavour continuously to maximize this experience of joy by pursuing those courses of action which they adjudge to be good.[5] A good action for Spinoza is simply that action which results in an experience of greater joy than any envisaged alternative, all things considered.[6]

In Spinoza's view, the activity of reasoning (our continuous endeavour to judge, on the basis of past experience, what is likely to happen to us—*vis à vis* our happiness—if we do x rather than y or z) is part and parcel of the activity of pursuing a good course of action. The reasoning and the activity which follows it make up a seamless whole.

Thus, on Spinoza's view, there is no room for the Kantian conception of an intervening exercise of will which is thought of as initiating our activities as distinct from the reasoning which foreshadows them.[7] He believes the seamless connection between reasoning and acting to be an empirical fact, so far as agents are concerned, and, as we will see in what immediately follows, all putative counter-examples to this empirical claim are subject to the same short rebuttal at Spinoza's hand.

To appreciate this, consider just what would count as an example of an agent's initially understanding that a given course of action would, so far as it can judge, maximize its happiness, but then not pursuing this line of endeavour.

Now it seems that there is no instance of human behaviour which would serve as such an example which would not at the same time make us doubt whether the person in question was possessed of a sound understanding. Given that no new factors intervene which serve to invalidate our subject's reasoning, how would we account for a failure to act in accordance with reasoning which seems sound to the person

---

[5] *Ethics*, pp. 136-137, III Proposition VI & Proposition IX Note; *cf.* III Proposition XXVIII & Proposition XXXIX Note.

[6] This rider is crucial, although in Spinoza's theory it goes without saying. Indeed it need not be said, given his understanding of human knowledge *viz*, that knowing is a relative matter, a continuous process of endeavouring to understand things from the widest possible perspective. So despite Spinoza's defining good as 'what is useful' this is not to be confused with any short-sighted pragmatism. The short-sighted view of what is useful does not tell us what is *truly* useful. What is truly useful to us is what is most productive of joy, for the individual certainly, but for an individual who is inextricably linked with all other individuals in the very terms of his or her endeavour. Moreover, joy is always greater, the wider the perspective from which the good action is adjudged to be good, since it is less likely, under such circumstances, that unforseen painful results will detract from the joy. See Fifth implication, p. 76 below.

[7] *Ethics*, p. 121 II Proposition XLIX Corollary: "The will and the understanding are one and the same."

engaged in it? As Spinoza quite rightly says in a similar context:

> If I am asked, whether such an one should not rather be considered an ass than a man; I answer that I do not know, neither do I know how a man should be considered, who hangs himself, or how we should consider children, fools, madmen, etc. (*Ethics*, p.126, II, Proposition XLIX Note.)

In short, inexplicable behaviour is not to be explained. Thus if we understand that people are agents, that agents' endeavours are explicable in terms of their judgments concerning the best way to increase their happiness, then, if we encounter beings whose behaviour is at odds with this picture, we have no real option other than to admit our inability to explain their behaviour. It seems our only recourse is to classify them as aberrant or sick agents—"fools, madmen, etc.".

What we must not do is to suppose that their inexplicable behaviour—their 'freedom' to go against their nature—exemplifies the essence of human agency. We must not conclude from the apparently inexplicable character of *their* behaviour that human agency in general is also inexplicable and then support this latter view by saying that human agents are, after all, *free* agents (where we introduce the notion of freedom to 'explain' the inexplicable). The defining feature of a class of things—those characteristics which make up its nominal essence—are always drawn from our observation of the normal behaviour of the things in question, not from aberrant behaviours. Thus it is simply a fact about normal human beings that their activities follow directly upon, indeed are simply an overt extension of, their reasoning concerning the way to maximize their happiness. Any gap between understanding and will is a sign that something is more or less wrong with the agent.

Scepticism with regard to the the rationality of human behaviour (where rationality is taken to be exemplified in cases where human beings attempt to maximize their happiness by using their understanding) seems to be a common response to Spinoza's fundamentally optimistic view of human agents as beings who cooperatively pursue happiness. Thus one can hear the sceptic offering a counter-example in this familiar fashion:[8] you say that human agents in the mass are rational cooperative beings motivated by a desire for mutual happiness. Why then do we not live in a harmonious world? And the short answer is that— speaking generally—we *do*, although there are still aberrant instances ("fools, madmen, etc."). These are aberrations from the norm of mature

---

[8] A good example of this sceptical view is provided in Kant's *CJ*, CtJ pp. 92-97, A 383-391 B 388-395.

human behaviour. Again, the sceptic may say: 'Why then do people not manage their endeavours more successfully the older they get, the more their reasoning improves?' and our answer is the same: speaking generally they *do*, although of course there are exceptions. In both cases there are numerous aberrations from the norm, but who would seriously argue that these aberrations are representative of the fate of human society in general, or of the course of the majority of individual human lives? The sober facts are that, normally, people (and the societies they constitute) *do* learn from experience. The error in regarding human endeavour as never getting anywhere lies very simply in taking instances of failure to learn as the norm. Certainly it is true that human improvement is only relative just as physical health is always relative. Misunderstandings, like sicknesses, do happen, but ill-considered endeavours (again, like sicknesses) can best be understood as aberrations from the norm or as exceptions to the rule of healthy understanding. To take the pathological examples of human endeavour (situations where our activities are not guided by our understanding and are thus rendered inexplicable) as the norm is to countenance the view that there is a gap between the understanding and the will which presents a fundamental barrier to any attempt to understand human activity. Moreover, as we have seen with Kant, to bridge this gap with the notion of freedom is, in the end, to render our behaviour equally inexplicable. For whether we freely choose to follow our understanding or (equally freely) choose to fly in the face of it, what this exercise actually amounts to remains a mystery.

Fifth Implication

A further implication of our mitigated agency is that the experience of being finite gives the human agent a perspective from which to view the activities of other agents. The agent will be conscious (through feelings of joy or sadness) of the contribution to, or frustration of, its agency which other agents bring about, and it will value another's agency from this perspective.

It follows from this that any finite agent (who understands the relationship between the understanding and the will) must regard another's behaviour, in so far as it leads to less reciprocity between agents, as stemming from ignorance on the part of the other agent. This carries the implication that this other person cannot be regarded as immoral or evil:

there is simply no room on this view of human activity for a moral judgment (a radical condemnation of the other) where people's actions are seen as stemming from the state of their understanding. People are 'good' (interact with others harmoniously) insofar as they are wise, and 'bad' insofar as they are ignorant (i.e. do not understand that their happiness lies in making common cause with others).[9]

What must be appreciated, if Spinoza's notion of human agency is to be accurately grasped, is that the metaphysical status of human agency is not amenable to a description under either of the traditional causal conceptions, viz. *autonomy* (in which the agent freely brings about its actions) or *heteronomy* (in which the agent's activities are naturally determined). (These are the options which exhaust the possibilities for explaining behaviour under the Kantian scheme.) Nor does the question of what one has to do to be good have only two possible answers: either that of the moralist (put all your efforts into willing to obey the categorical imperative) or that of the naturalist (do nothing special, just follow your nature). Under Spinoza's conception of agency as finite, what we can do to be good is not totally within our power, nor is it completely outside our power. There is something we can do and there are techniques (even if they are often indirect) which we can practise which will improve our chances of success in our endeavour to be good. These techniques reflect the essential finitude of the human agent and are designed to help one to follow the injunction appropriate to a finite agent, viz. do your best.

For Spinoza, human agents exist in so far as they act, but their actions are tied to their understanding and it, in turn, as *human* understanding, is always only more or less adequate due to its finitude. The relative success of an endeavouring agent is therefore a function of

---

[9] It may be asked: What about 'culpable ignorance'? Clearly we blame people for not knowing or understanding certain things which we feel a normal person should understand, for example, that drinking and driving must be kept apart. The Spinozist must insist in such cases that, although normal people should be aware of such strictures, when their behaviour does not exhibit an awareness of them (when they drink and then drive) the blame we assign to them, and the punishments we levy, can only be designed to raise their level of understanding so that the next time they will not forget. For the Spinozist, the actual commission of the crime (drinking and driving) is still not a deliberate act (an act of free will). It is an act which flows from the state of the person's understanding at the time and since it is determined in this way, it cannot be subject to a moral condemnation since it was not brought about by a free choice. For the Spinozist there is never any sense to the claim that the person could have done otherwise.

the relative adequacy of the understanding which guides it. Furthermore, whether we believe that there is something we can actively do to promote our endeavours or whether we think that this is beyond our deliberate control is itself a function of the understanding we have of our agency and our situation. We can therefore distinguish two states in which a human being may endeavour: the first is that state in which the agent *implicitly* understands the nature of its agency, the second is that state in which this understanding is *explicit*.

In the first state the agent remains (more or less) in bondage, specifically in bondage to its emotions.[10] In childhood this bondage is evident and virtually total. Growing up is the process of gradually learning how to temper our emotional responses (and thus our behaviour) in the light of past experience. With rare exceptions, those who grow up come to an intuitive or implicit understanding of how, for the most part, to control their responses to their emotional reactions. However, in such a state, every advance in our capacity to control our responses is gained only through those lessons which experience happens to teach us. The experience of a lifetime might well be too short to bring that implicit capacity for controlling our responses, and thus our agency, to the point where we would feel ourselves to be more, rather than less, in control of our agency.

The second state of endeavour is that in which the agent has come to grasp explicitly the finite nature of its agency. Through understanding the nature of human agency, people can come to a conscious appreciation of various well-known techniques which can then be put into practice on a regular basis in order to increase their control over their responses to the occurrence of their emotional reactions.

One such technique turns on our coming to appreciate how the efficacy of our understanding can be increased by actually tracing out in our imagination the likely consequences of various lines of action.[11] Spinoza's idea here is that our present emotions (which determine our behaviour, other things being equal) need to be validated, so to speak, by envisaging in an imaginative (active) way what is likely to happen if we act in accordance with them. This process brings to light any disutilities involved in the various courses of action which our emotions motivate us to take, and these will be manifest in terms of the emotional distress we will feel as we contemplate our projected activity. Such emotions, born of our imaginative projections, will serve to counter the strength of those

---

[10] This is Spinoza's terminology. See *Ethics*, p. 187, IV Preface.

[11] *Ethics*, pp. 252-254, V Proposition X Note.

naturally occurring emotions which prompt us toward a given line of action, thus giving us power to alter the direction of our lives. Spinoza is here pointing out that we cannot consistently succeed as agents unless we are consistently active. And we cannot be consistently active unless our understanding of the nature of our agency (our understanding of what actually motivates our behaviour and how it can be influenced) informs each exercise of it.

Another technique rests on the idea that our positive emotions are a function of our understanding of the situation which arouses them.[12] In general, when Spinoza considers the power reason has over negative or passive emotions, he says that the more we are able to understand the necessary nature of a given situation, the less we will suffer from negative emotions which always flow from an inadequate understanding of our situation. By way of example, he points out

> that pain arising from the loss of any good is mitigated, as soon as the man who has lost it perceives, that it could not by any means have been preserved. (*Ethics*, p. 250, V Proposition VI Note)

A third technique recognizes the fact that it is hard to think clearly when we are agitated by some negative emotion. If we are to deal with the situations which arouse such emotions effectively, we must have previously prepared ourselves so that we can immediately recognize a fresh situation as one which is best dealt with according to a particular trusted maxim. That we may accomplish this, in Spinoza's words:

> that this precept of reason may be always ready to our hand in time of need [in this case the precept is that hatred is to be conquered by love or generosity, and is not to be met with hatred in return], we should often think over and reflect upon the wrongs generally committed by men, and in what manner and way they may be best warded off by highmindedness: we shall thus associate the idea of the wrong with the idea of this precept, which accordingly will always be ready for use when a wrong is done to us. (*Ethics*, p. 253, V Proposition X Note)

Salvation is Spinoza's term for what we seek when, even in the *implicit* state of endeavour, we see a difference between being controlled and being in control and want to be more often in the latter state. We wish to be 'saved' from the things which hold us in bondage, viz. our

---

[12] *Ethics*, p. 171, III Proposition LVIII and LIX including Note.

emotions, and we long for some means to increase our control over our behaviour so that we are not so frustratingly dependent upon the chance of fresh experience to teach us greater control the hard way. We have just such a means (the techniques which we have ready-to-hand) when we reach an explicit understanding of the nature of human agency. These techniques are in fact familiar to us even when our understanding of them is only implicit. As Spinoza says, there are "remedies against the emotions, which I believe all have had experience of."[13] But he notes that, though familiar through experience, all people "do not accurately observe or distinctly see [them]."[14]

His view is that it is only through this explicit process that we can come to an attitude of mind through which we will consistently increase our control over our endeavours. Because our agency—our will—is only as active as our understanding, the only thing we can do to improve our behaviour, to make it more active and more satisfying, is to improve our understanding. This can be done only when we "accurately observe" and "distinctly see" how these remedies actually work.

This is a crucial insight in that, without a clear—an explicit—appreciation of how the will works as a function of the understanding, we can come to imagine, as Kant did, that the will can be exercised on its own, so to speak, independently of our understanding of the situation in which we are acting. We can thus come to imagine that we can govern our affects (emotions) and thus our endeavours by the pure exercise of our will. As Spinoza remarks of the Stoics:

[they] have thought, that the emotions depended absolutely on our will, and that we could absolutely govern them. But these philosophers were compelled, by the protest of experience, not from their own principles, to confess, that no slight practice and zeal is needed to control and moderate them. (*Ethics*, p. 244, V Preface)

So for Spinoza living more actively is a matter of applying techniques—a matter of practice. In his words:

Whosoever will diligently observe and practise these precepts [*his techniques*] (which indeed are not difficult) will verily, in a short space of time, be able, *for the most part*, to direct his actions according to the commandments of reason [his understanding]. (*Ethics*, p. 254, V Proposition X Note, our italics)

---

[13] *Ethics*, p. 247, V Preface.
[14] *loc.cit.*

Nor is there any 'Catch-22' in this with respect to *how* one is to acquire the 'will-power' to follow Spinoza's advice. Once you have understood how the understanding and the will are connected, by that very fact you will have the will to improve your understanding.[15]

Finally, before turning to Kant's conception of agency it is important to note that a life that is governed by an adequate understanding of the nature of our powers as agents is characterized by Spinoza as a life of freedom. This freedom is a relative freedom from the bondage of the emotions, a freedom that is realized in varying degrees as our understanding of the nature of our agency becomes steadily more explicit. Spinoza's injunction to finite agents who understand the nature of their agency has, therefore, a relative character: to endeavour to do well (i.e. the best you can) and to rejoice.[16]

---

[15] There is a catch but it is not of the Catch-22 variety. Your will to improve your understanding will be *proportional* to your appreciation (the depth of your understanding) of the link between the understanding and the will.

[16] *Ethics*, p. 221, IV Proposition L Note.

CHAPTER SIX

AGENCY IN KANT

A study of Kant reveals three distinct characterizations of human agency, three distinct ways in which a human being can be said to be active. These characterizations find expression respectively in the three *Critiques*, each of which focuses on a different area of human experience. In the *Critique of Pure Reason*, the agent is credited with a transcendental capacity to process (categorize) the raw materials supplied by our sensible intuition into experience:

> The manifold of representations can be given in an intuition which is purely sensible, that is, nothing but receptivity; and the form of this intuition can lie *a priori* in our faculty of representation, without being anything more than the mode in which the subject is affected. But the combination (*conjunctio*) of a manifold in general can never come to us though the senses, and cannot, therefore, be already contained in the pure form of sensible intuition. For it is an act of spontaneity of the faculty of representation; and since this faculty, to distinguish it from sensibility, must be entitled understanding, all combination—be we conscious of it or not, be it a combination of the manifold of intuition, empirical or non-empirical, or of various concepts—is an act of the understanding. To this act the general title 'synthesis' may be assigned, as indicating that we cannot represent to ourselves anything as combined in the object which we have not ourselves previously combined, and that of all representations *combination* is the only one which cannot be given through objects. Being an act of the self-activity of the subject, it cannot be executed save by the subject itself. It will be easily observed that this action is originally one and is equipollent for all combination, and that its dissolution, namely, *analysis,* which appears to be its opposite, yet always presupposes it. For where the understanding has not previously combined, it cannot dissolve, since only as having been combined *by the understanding* can anything that allows of analysis be given to the faculty of representation. (*CPR*, pp.151-152, B 129-130)

Note that this processing is described by Kant as being "an act of the self-activity of the subject," "an act of spontaneity of the faculty of representation." The mechanics of this spontaneous processing consist in applying to intuition the Pure Concepts of the Understanding (the Categories). What this amounts to becomes clearer when we note that for Kant a concept is a rule.[1] The Pure Concepts of the Understanding are then rules which intuitions must obey when they are combined, if the result is to yield a knowable experience. Now part of what Kant means when he asserts that we follow these rules *spontaneously* is that we are not aware of doing so. We only know that we engage in this spontaneous activity through a transcendental deduction of the conditions required to make a (knowable) experience possible. Thus we have no direct experience of ourselves as engaged in this activity, in the paradigmatic sense of being aware of ourselves as controlling an activity in that variable way which gives the notion of 'control' its meaning. That is, in our spontaneous application of the Categories we are not involved in a way of acting which has a value[2] varying with the amount of effort[3] we put into it.

In sum, Kant's transcendental characterization of human agency in the first Critique rules it out as a vehicle for generating value.

The second characterization of human agency to be considered is presented in the *Critique of Judgment*. Here agency takes on a hybrid character: the spontaneous capacity to generate aesthetic judgments is joined with a capacity to safeguard the purity of the judgments concerned. Kant thinks that when we make an aesthetic judgment ('This is beautiful') we are reporting the fact that we are experiencing a certain feeling which is the sign that a certain kind of mental activity (a judgment) is taking place in response to a given intuition. This activity is spontaneous in that we are not aware of being able to control the

---

[1] *CPR*, p. 135, A 106: "But a concept is always, as regards its form, something universal which serves as a rule."

[2] That controlled activity is a value-generating phenomenon is evident from the following considerations. When we are aware of being more or less in control we are *ipso facto* aware of being more or less successfully engaged in our endeavours. There is therefore a value which is tied directly to the degree to which we feel ourselves to be succeeding (or failing) in controlling the exercise of our agency. So in the present case no value attaches to the spontaneous exercise of our agency in processing intuitions into experiences. This is not an activity which we can do well or badly.

[3] 'Effort' means no more than the sense we have of deliberately increasing our control over our activity, i.e. exercising our agency more actively by attending with greater care to what we are doing—and we do this as a consequence of experiencing some relevant desire which provides us with the motive for taking this greater care.

activity which generates this response. We cannot, therefore, take any credit for the delight we experience as the sign that we have made one of these spontaneous judgments of beauty. But an element of control—and therefore credit—can enter into such judgments in so far as we regard ourselves as being under an obligation to ensure that our judgments remain free of utilitarian or moral interests.[4] If an aesthetic judgment is to be kept pure it must not be affected by such irrelevant considerations as, for example, the moral lesson depicted in a religious painting. Once the rules for maintaining the purity of an aesthetic judgment are understood, the observance of these rules is something we can endeavour to control. We can therefore be held responsible for the purity of our aesthetic judgments. People can attempt, with a greater or lesser degree of success, to maintain the purity of their aesthetic judgings. As a consequence this aspect of aesthetic judging fits the paradigm of an exercise of agency: we can be aware of what we should be doing and of exercising our capacity to this end more or less diligently.

It is however still the case that after attempting to abide by the canons of aesthetic judging we still have no control over whether we will experience beauty (aesthetic delight) on perceiving a given object. This experience will be spontaneously generated only if the conditions which alone can spark it off are in fact present. (In Kant's view the experience of beauty will occur only if there is scope in what we experience for the faculties of the understanding and the imagination to engage in an harmonious free play, for it is the free play of these faculties which generates the characteristic feeling of disinterested delight which in turn prompts us to attribute aesthetic value to a given experience.[5])

It is important to recognize in this connection that two quite distinct types of value are involved in an instance of aesthetic judging. The first is the natural pleasure (or displeasure) that characterizes the feeling we have when, due to the free (or constrained) interplay of the faculties, we experience beauty (or its opposite). This value is generated spontaneously and its occurrence is outside the agent's control. The second kind of value has a quasi-moral character (using the term 'moral' as Kant uses it). This derives from the pleasure which we feel when we have more or less successfully avoided contaminating the purity of our aesthetic judgings by carefully attending to the precepts which serve to distinguish such

---

[4] "One must not be in the least prepossessed in favour of the real existence of the thing, but must preserve complete indifference in this respect, in order to play the part of judge in matters of taste." *CJ*, CaJ p. 43, BA 6.

[5] See *CJ*, CaJ pp. 58-60, BA 28-32

judgings from their closely related cousins (judgings pertaining to the charm an object has for us or its utility or its moral interest). This pleasure then is pleasure that attaches to our sense that we have done something properly (according to the accepted rules). To characterize this kind of value as quasi-moral is to emphasize the fact that there is a right way to go about making aesthetic judgments, if one's object is to maintain the purity of these activities. However they are only *quasi-moral* because no one thinks that he or she actually has a *moral* duty to keep aesthetic judgments pure.

The quasi-moral character of this value may be further illustrated by reference to the curious contempt in which the aesthete is held by (and in which he or she—in turn—holds) the masses. This contempt is doubtless a function of the fact that such a person treats the observance of aesthetic canons of judgment as an end in itself, thus giving a moral status to an activity which has no recognized moral value.[6] Moreover, the 'moral' confusion into which the aesthete falls is not easy to avoid since, for example, the business of trying to maintain the purity of one's aesthetic judgings is subject to the very same difficulty as the moral agent's efforts to act purely, to act solely out of the thought of duty. Just as a moral interest (or considerations relating to the charm or utility of the object in question) may secretly intrude on, and thus undetectably contaminate, the purity of an aesthetic judging, so too a prudential consideration may unconsciously motivate and thus spoil the purity of an ostensibly dutiful action.

It is worth noting that, in both cases, the same tendency (which can with some justice be regarded as pathological) is at work, viz. the notion that one can obtain absolute control over one's activities, a tendency firmly rooted in the Kantian idea that the value of aesthetic or moral activities will be completely eradicated if they are in any degree sullied by non-aesthetic or non-moral considerations. With this in mind it becomes quite clear how Kant's conception of agency differs from Spinoza's. For Spinoza, the value that accrues to an exercise of one's agency is not dependent upon whether that exercise is pure or not. Rather it turns on the relative increase (or decrease) in control that one experiences in the exercise of one's agency. For a finite agent (who understands that it is finite) the idea that it might exercise complete control over its activities (engage in, e.g. a *pure* aesthetic, or *pure* moral activity) is no more than an idle piece of silliness. It is idle because there is no way of

---

[6] Cf. the view many have of people who treat grammatical rules as absolute, as having almost a moral character.

ascertaining the purity of one's motives and silly because it flies in the face of our finitude. We could never completely[7] understand any situation which demands action on our part, so that, necessarily, our action can only have a value relative to the degree of our understanding of the situation. The better we understand it, the greater the value which attaches to our activity with respect to it. However in every case we can only do our best and this is never the same as doing what is right in the absolute sense which Kant attaches to this notion.

In short, then, the value which Spinoza finds in 'doing our best' is not a moral value. It is a value which is intrinsic to the direction (the increase or decrease in our control of our agency) in which we feel ourselves to be developing as we engage in the business of living. For Spinoza, all activities have an intrinsic value (they are done well or badly) which reflects the level of our endeavour as finite agents.

We now come to Kant's third characterization of agency (contained in the *Critique of Practical Reason*)—agency in the moral sphere. We noted above that aesthetic judging has a quasi-moral aspect in that we have a 'responsibility' to keep our aesthetic judgments free of moral or utilitarian interest if we wish to keep them pure. And the presumption here is that we do want to keep them pure simply because, if we do not, such judgments would cease to be aesthetic judgments: a faculty we possess would not be exercised properly, and we would be the poorer for it.

We also noted that the distinctive thing about our capacity to make aesthetic judgments was that, if we followed the rules which serve to

---

[7] Kant would say that the Categorical Imperative sanctions moral laws which can be completely understood and therefore sanctions actions which have an absolute worth. However, the reason that action does not necessarily follow from the contemplation of such laws is that the 'knowledge' that we have when we completely understand the moral law is analytic. It is knowledge of the meaning of words—of the internal logic of forms of life (like lying and promise-keeping). As analytic, it tells us nothing which connects us with the world. It cannot serve as a guide to action simply because it only states a rule. Aristotle was right when, in discussing the practical syllogism, he pointed out that as well as a rule (the major Premiss), you need knowledge that a particular situation facing you falls under that rule, and you have to accept that the rule applies to you before any action will ensue ('Nichomachean Ethics', translated by Sir David Ross, in *The Basic Works of Aristotle*, ed. Richard McKeon, Random House, New York, 1941, p. 1041, 1147a 29ff). In Kant's theory, a person has to freely decide whether they are going to apply this rule to themselves, in a given instance, but how we make such a decision is, as Kant always admits, inexplicable. And we contend that it is, in the end, impossible to understand why an inexplicable decision-making procedure should have an absolute worth.

maintain the purity of aesthetic judgments, such judgments will spontaneously occur when an appropriate intuition is present. The point to bear in mind, then, is that, although I can do something to ensure that aesthetic judgments are aesthetic in character, I cannot do anything to control the actual occurrence of aesthetic delight: this will either happen or it will not, depending on the nature of the stimulus.

Now in the case of moral activities, I have a technique, provided by the categorical imperative which, if followed, will ensure that the maxim of my projected behaviour will be a moral maxim. But this moral validation of my maxim does not mean that any behaviour I spontaneously engage in (which happens to satisfy this maxim) will be an act with moral value.[10] To give it moral value I must do it *because* it conforms to the maxim, that is, I must do it out of duty, and I can only do it out of duty if I freely engage myself to do it for duty's sake: moral action must therefore stem from the free exercise of our agency.

Now to characterize agency—in so far as moral activities are concerned—as free, is to characterize the control which we exercise over it as absolute. This, however, immediately allows for the possibility of attributing to such absolute exercises of agency a kind of value which is quite distinct from the 'everyday' value which is associated with getting better and better at doing things. To see this, let us review the relationship between the exercise of our agency in general and the character of the value that attaches to it. We have put forward the view that the paradigmatic notion of agency is that of a capacity through which we can exercise a varying degree of control over what we do. With our awareness of a variable capacity for control, we also have, *ipso facto,* the notion of doing better or worse, of succeeding or failing in our various endeavours. We have, thus, the notion of a value that is tied directly to the degree to which we feel ourselves to be succeeding (or failing) in controlling the exercise of our agency: the greater our sense of actively controlling our affairs, the greater the value we place upon our activity and therefore on our being as agents. This value stems ultimately from the simple fact that when we exercise a relatively increased control of our agency we experience a sense of satisfaction with ourselves.

This close relationship between the relatively active (controlled) exercise of one's agency and the feelings of satisfaction which grace such

---

[10] This is in contrast with the case of spontaneous aesthetic judgments which happen to conform to the rules for making pure judgments. Such judgments are still aesthetic in character despite the fact that their being pure was the result of a spontaneous judgment not the result of trying to obey the rules for making pure aesthetic judgments.

endeavours thus provides a natural and uncomplicated basis for assessing whether, as human agents, we are at any given time flourishing. However, the logic of this notion of flourishing is open-ended. I cannot flourish and be done with it. If I am to flourish at all I must keep on flourishing: a continuous effort is required. This continuous struggle to increase our control over our behaviour (for only an increase in our control over our activity will bring that sense of satisfaction with our being that assures us that we are flourishing) presents us with a price that must always be paid if we are to gain the satisfaction associated with human flourishing. The enigma that surrounds our understanding of our agency is closely bound up with our not knowing—in any straightforward way—how to pay this price and thus not being able to flourish in anything more than that episodic fashion that common experience shows to be the norm for human endeavour.

The usual practical solutions to this problem have always relied on various sorts of rewards and punishments aimed at coercing our agency externally, so to speak. However such carrot-and-stick practices inevitably reduce our activity to the status of an effect brought about by an external cause, whereas the essence of the special satisfaction which attaches itself to any active endeavour lies in the fact that the agents in question *brought themselves* to do what they did. How then can people learn to exercise their agency so that their activity will be increasingly self-directed?

Kant's views on this subject are important. He made perhaps his principal contribution to ethical theory by clearly recognizing that it is this self-directing feature of human agency that gives human endeavour its unique capacity to create moral value. However, he insisted that unless we ourselves were the *exclusive* cause of what we did, then our endeavours would be bereft of that special feeling of satisfaction ('self-contentment') which is the hallmark of that exercise of human agency which creates moral value.

Such an 'either/or' view of agency—that it is *either* exclusively determined by external causes *or* exclusively self-determined—presents a problem. The problem is this: we suggested that the value we attach to our endeavours was relative to the degree of control which we exercise over our behaviour. The more active our endeavours, the more we feel ourselves to be flourishing as agents. The implication of such a view is that flourishing, as a way of being that is marked by a relative increase in one's active control over one's behaviour, is an asymptotic process. In other words, we, as separate and distinct individuals, can never be fully active. The value that we experience through our activities is based on the experience of a relative increase or decrease in our activity as agents. We can be *better or worse* as agents, but never *good or bad* (completely active, or completely passive).

And yet Kant, in supposing that the uniqueness of a moral value was a function of such completely active exercises of our agency (so-called 'free acts of will'), leaves no logical room for asking questions about how to increase one's capacity to will purely or freely. Acts of will on his view are *either* pure (free) *or* determined. Thus Kantian agents cannot get better at being good. Each action is an all-or-nothing affair with respect to the value which accrues to it. Thus in contrast with the ordinary case, the realization of this absolute value depends ultimately on whether or not (not to what *degree*) a person exercises his or her agency in an act of will which incorporates or deliberately ignores the moral option (the action sanctioned by the Categorical Imperative).

It is therefore our contention that this move from relative values to absolute or moral values is a function of Kant's idea that human agency can be exercised in a completely controlled, and thus free, act of will. We must now consider what phenomena, what features of human experience, led him to believe this. What explanation is there for the fact that he took up, with such conviction, a position in which the ultimate basis for all that is worthwhile is a totally inscrutable capacity freely to direct our behaviour?

In the next chapter we will look at this question by considering the phenomena which Kant uses to persuade his audience that an absolutist view of agency is credible, if not explicable. In the case of each of these phenomena (which seemed to Kant to be evidence for the existence of a moral dimension in human life) we will offer an agent-naturalistic explanation, thereby suggesting that this moral dimension is illusory.

CHAPTER SEVEN

EXPLAINING AWAY THE EVIDENCE FOR MORALITY AS A FORM OF LIFE

Kant finds in certain phenomena evidence that we can legitimately regard ourselves as capable of engaging in the moral form of life. As we take note of these phenomena in this chapter we will argue that there is a naturalistic explanation for each of them. We can account for their presence in our experience in a way that effectively explains away the special character which, for Kant, marked them as uniquely *moral* phenomena. To prepare the way, however, we must first set out what the term 'naturalistic explanation' is intended to signify when it follows the Spinozistic model.

This can be accomplished by differentiating three sorts of relationships between cause and effect which a person may appeal to in the course of offering an explanation. The first causal relationship provides a naturalistic explanation of some event in the sense that the relation between the effect and the cause that explains it is drawn from our experience of the apparently invariable course of nature. In such a case, an event's occurrence is explained in Humean fashion by pointing to the cause, i.e. the event which regularly precedes it. The second causal relationship involves the notion of agent-causality. In this kind of explanation, a central causal role is accorded to the agent who is thought of as exercising a variable degree of control over the activity for which an explanation is being sought. Where agent-causality is invoked in order to explain the occurrence of some event, we are inclined to regard such explanations as naturalistic in so far as they appeal to our past experience as agents acting to bring about certain effects in a regular—if not completely invariable—way. This qualification reflects the finite or limited nature of an agent's control over its activities. As finite, an agent cannot exercise an absolute control. Thus the causal efficacy of its control can only be predicted in a general way.

The idea that we are always only more or less in control of our activities provides us with the notion of a continuum of control. This idea of a continuum allows us to place the first kind of naturalistic explanation at one of the theoretical ends of this continuum. Thus if an agent were to exercise no control over its activities, if it were to be completely passive (to use Spinoza's terminology), the explanation of what happens to it would depend entirely on the character of the preceding states of affairs. No activity—no willing we might say—on the part of the agent could be regarded as contributing to the causal conditions which account for what happens to it. In this case the explanation of what happens to it would be governed by Humean constraints.

At the other end of the continuum we have a theoretical position in which the agent exercises unlimited control over its activities. Here the explanation of what brought about the action may be described, quite fairly, as supernatural. Thus, where the agent *alone* is considered responsible for what happens, the effect is not deemed to be caused by any power which is contingent upon an empirical, i.e. natural, state of affairs. Thus where absolute control is said to be exercised, an explanation for this can only be attributed to the agent's possession of a power which can bring about some natural effect from outside nature, as it were.

A free will is such a 'supernatural' power. Agents who believe that they possess such a free power will then explain their actions by reference to it and when they do so, the supernaturalistic flavour of their explanation will be evident in that they will not refer to any preceding empirical states of affairs in order to explain *how* they did what they did. It will then seem a kind of mystery—both to the agent and to others—how an agent is thus enabled, save by reference to his or her possession of a free will. An explanation in terms of free willing will seem, therefore, to be an explanation that explains nothing and this is simply because there is such a close tie between the notion of explaining something and naturalistic reconstructions of *how* an event came about.[1]

Implicit in this analysis of these three types of explanation as lying on a continuum is the consideration that if one end-point—supernaturalism—is, ordinarily, not regarded as providing a real explanation (as an end-point it is simply a limiting case of an explanation and as such not an explanation at all), then by the same token the other end-point—Humean naturalism—should also be regarded as empty of explanatory power. And indeed it can be so characterized.[2]

---

[1] See pp. 14 *ff.* above.
[2] And it is continually so characterized by, for example, the three-year-

Thus although we can say that water freezes at 273K and 101.1 kPa, this explanation does not tell us *why* this is so. The laws which govern physical events simply describe what, in fact, happens under a given set of circumstances. There is no explanation as to why the law holds, only a description stating that this is how, in fact, things are. In practice this is, of course, all we expect a scientific or mechanistic explanation to provide. It is only the young child—whose intuitive sense of what a proper explanation should amount to stems from his or her own operations upon the environment—who expects anything more. For the child a proper explanation must be concluded in terms of agent-causality: it must accommodate both the 'how' and the 'why' of an event's coming about. For us, as adults, our intuitive sense of what a really satisfying explanation should be also stems from this intuitive demand.

It is on the basis of this common intuition that we have noted that the explanations at either end of the continuum cannot be said really to explain anything. This is simply a consequence of the fact that agent-explanation is the intuitive paradigm of what a satisfying explanation amounts to. Physical naturalism explains how things happen ('This is just how things are arranged') but not why. Supernaturalism explains why things happen (through reference to acts of will of some person or a God) but not how. But both the 'how' and the 'why' are present in an agent-explanation because agent-causality, as revealed in finite creatures such as human beings, is adequately grasped only when actions are viewed as stemming partially from necessary preconditions (which provide the means—the 'how' of accomplishing something) and partially from an agent's having an end in view, a desire to achieve a certain satisfaction (which provides the motive, the 'why' of the deed). Combining both views we can adequately conceive the action as involving interaction between the particular agent's desires (and capabilities) and the circumstances which circumscribe its actions.

To round out this sketch of agent-explanations, we need to add a note concerning the correct understanding of the Spinozistic characterization of agent-causality. When actions are represented as stemming partially from an agent's desiring some end and partially from the circumstances which influence the execution of this end, it may appear that the Spinozistic approach does no more than compartmentalize agents into active and passive elements. That is, it may seem that, as agents, we are held to have a passive (deterministic) element which plays a greater or lesser part

---

old with his or her incessant 'But why?' questions.

in determining our actions, according to the degree to which the active (free) element is exercised. However, such a view places an undue emphasis on the will as being the controlling factor in which the real explanation of our behaviour lies: on this view the degree to which we (somehow) exercise our will determines how much room, so to speak, is left for the passive (deterministic) side of us to play its part in our behaviour. This approach is unsatisfactory because it amounts to converting the agent-explanation into a supernatural-explanation (i.e. the real explanation of the event's coming about rests on an explanation of why it came about, viz. through an exercise of the will). Such a pure 'why' explanation is inadequate because it locates the cause of our activity solely in the notion of an independent will controlling our behaviour in an inexplicable or supernatural fashion. This is a false picture of agent-causality according to Spinoza.

Spinoza's more complex account of agent-causality offers a different conception of the active and passive elements which go into our make-up. In Spinoza's view, human activity is a process which is characterized not as *either* controlled *or* determined, but instead as more or less active, more or less controlled or deliberate. And the factor which determines the extent of the agent's control is the relative success of its endeavours to understand its situation.

As we have seen,[3] the process of endeavouring to understand can occur implicitly or explicitly. When it occurs implicitly, my past experience guides my behaviour more or less automatically. Under such circumstances I feel less in control of my behaviour, more a creature of habit, being led by my past experience. On the other hand, when I actively employ my understanding, when I explicitly think a thing through with the awareness that I can thus increase my control over my activities, I feel that, to that degree, I am the cause of my behaviour. Thus it is in these cases of the explicit exercise of our agency (*via* various techniques[4]) that we feel our actions are explicable in terms of what we are actively doing. We feel that our behaviour is self-explanatory under such circumstances (we have the desire, we work out the best means of achieving the satisfaction of the desire and act accordingly) and it is because of this that we recognize the paradigmatic character of explanations which rely on this Spinozistic characterization of agency.[5]

---

[3] See pp. 78 *ff.*, above.

[4] *loc.cit.*

[5] The inadequacy of explanations which rely on either the Humean or the Kantian characterizations, the extreme ends of the continuum, is, once again, made clear by the reactions of young children. They can take only

In explicit instances of agent-causality, the how and the why of my behaviour, and their essential interconnection, are evident in the fact that my willing finds its basis in the active character of my efforts to understand the situation I am in. Willing and understanding come to be seen as aspects of a single process, a process which explains my behaviour by effectively constituting it.

This has been a rather lengthy digression, but in the project before us—citing those phenomena which Kant regards as *prima facie* evidence for the existence of a moral form of life and showing how they may be given an agent-naturalistic explanation—it is important that the reader should have a clear notion of what we mean by an agent-naturalistic explanation.

What, then, are the phenomena which convinced Kant that the moral form of life was a real possibility and not the product of mere "high-flown fancy." [6]? There are six and we will now consider each in turn.

The Good Will

Kant first cites the widespread, indeed universal opinion of humankind, that only a good will is good without qualification.[7] His argument is that if we discount the effects of good-willing, if we imagine that for some contingent reason the good-willing of some agent does not translate into good deeds, we still regard the willing—just in itself—as intrinsically valuable. As he puts it,

> ...and if even the greatest effort should not avail it to achieve anything of its end, and if there remained only the good will (not as a mere wish but as the summoning of all the means in our power), it would sparkle like a jewel with its own light, as something that had its full worth in itself. (*FMM*, p. 56, AB 3)

There is no doubt that this characterization of our attitudes towards

---

so much of the Humean response: "That's just the way things are." (an attempt to put an end to their 'how?' questioning) and are equally likely to balk at the Kantian response: "Because I say so." (an attempt to end their 'why?' questioning). What they really want is an explanation which demonstrates the natural interconnection of things and which at the same time relates them to this system of nature in such a way that their experience of their own agency serves to explain why the system works the way it does.

[6] *FFM*, p. 56, BA 4.
[7] *FFM*, pp. 55-56, BA 1-2.

people who intend and try to do what is right—even though they are frustrated in their endeavours and fail to accomplish anything—is correct. We value, for itself, any attempt to do what is right. But can we conclude that our *unconditional* admiration for this quality of a person indicates that this quality is really unconditionally good? Kant's argument presents the matter as if it were a conclusion which followed virtually by definition. Thus if we proceed by saying that good willing can (*ex hypothesi*) sometimes be fruitless,[8] we must conclude that, if on such occasions we still accord praise to it, it must have an unconditional value of its own. This will be so by definition, since a value can be said to be unconditional if it is valued irrespective of its utility value. The value which then attaches to good willing *must* be unconditional (*ex hypothesi*) since it does not result in activities which have utility value, but is, for all that, still regarded as valuable.

But can we confidently accept this common view (that seems to make it virtually a matter of definition) that utility value can actually be quite irrelevant to the value of an act of will? It is worth pausing here a moment to consider what our strategy really is in posing this question.

At first it may seem that our aim is to show Kant up as simply begging the question. It may appear that we wish to show that Kant's argument is based on the bald assertion that, as an incontestable empirical fact, people value the willing of what is right, even when (as happens on certain occasions) there is a lack of valuable consequences (i.e. the act proves to have no utility value). This being so, it would then be our strategy to cite some recalcitrant empirical data as counter-examples which demonstrate that utility value *is* present in such cases and serves to disprove Kant's empirical contention. For example we might point out that we invariably take pleasure in instances of good willing because we can appreciate, imaginatively, the utility values of the consequences of such an act should it have come to fruition. But it is apparent that such a strategy is quite useless as a means of combatting Kant's argument. For every bit of recalcitrant data we may cite, Kant can always respond: but suppose that on some occasion this utility value were not actually brought into existence by the good willing? Is it not still the case that we would value the willing in question—just in itself? What are we to reply?

The apparent force of Kant's rejoinder lies in his assuming the existence of a theoretical 'we' who always value such acts of will in and for themselves. This serves to supply a universal character to the

---

[8] *FFM*, p. 56, AB 3.

evaluation since the theoretical 'we' responsible for such assessments is always deemed to be capable of recognizing value in such activities in a completely disinterested fashion (i.e. ignoring any utility values as irrelevant). And the attribution of unconditional value to acts of will needs just such a foundation. For if 'we' were not disinterested when we evaluated the worth of such acts of will, it would follow that the value we attributed to the act in question would be a function of our *experiencing* it as valuable. In such a case, it is clear that the value of the act would not be independent of our interests, not an unconditional value.

How then can Kant simply assume the possibility of such disinterested assessments of value? To appreciate the problem such a view involves, consider the following line of thought. What is it that gives the form of life we call 'valuing' its intelligibility in relation to our experience? The experiential constituent of valuing is a positive emotional state, a state which is the origin of our very concept of value. Given this fact, it seems fair to ask: what would it be like to recognize an activity as valuable, without at the same time experiencing its value in terms of a positive emotional response? The logic of this form of life simply does not permit me to discount or ignore the positive emotional response (the feelings) involved in valuing something. It does not permit me to regard a thing's value as being quite independent of my recognizing this value in emotional terms. In other words, the notion of something as valuable *in itself* is at odds with the form of life in which the concept of value is embedded: we value things because we perceive them as having value and we perceive them as having value through experiencing a positive emotional response to them. An 'in-itself' value has, therefore, no intelligible basis in an ordinary understanding of valuing. To give it a basis, a new form of life has to be assumed which would then serve as a context in which this essentially new kind of valuing could be understood. As a consequence, our argument against Kant's 'empirical' contention that there is something which can be regarded as good in itself (any instance of good willing) is not an argument which contends that *within the moral form of life*—no one in fact values good willing for its own sake. (In other words it is not an argument that says anything about the empirical facts once the moral form of life is up and running.) It is an argument intended to show only that the intelligibility of Kant's empirical contention rests entirely on an *a priori* 'fact', viz. that 'we' ('in fact') recognize the existence of unconditional moral values, values which are good in themselves and that *this* therefore constitutes *prima facie empirical* evidence for the existence of the moral form of life as a robust phenomenon. Kant's reasoning here is circular because an independent acknowledgment of the intelligibility of 'in-itself' valuing is required before the existence of this value can be used as the *ratio cognoscendi*[9]—the basis of our knowledge—of morality as a real form of life (as opposed to its existence as a mere high-flown fancy).

If the above argument presented the whole story, it would seem to follow that no one could actually understand the notion of something as valuable in itself. However, people do seem to understand this notion quite adequately and make use of it as a standard or ideal of goodness. We can therefore only conclude that the form of life which makes moral value intelligible is already in place and fully operational as a highly complex system of interdependent concepts and phenomena. As a result, it may well be that its overall intelligibility may be harder to call into question because of the fact that the various elements of this form of life, *in their mutual interconnections*, strengthen the overall claim of morality to be regarded as a legitimate form of life. Thus each element (the sum of which constitutes the evidence for the existence of morality as a form of life) supports the credibility of all the others by providing them with a context which is the basis of their mutual intelligibility. In this chapter we are considering these elements one by one, following our plan of citing an agent-naturalistic explanation for each of them which will serve to explain them away. However the overall resilience of the combination of elements which together constitute morality (as a form of life) will prove a continuing problem for such a piecemeal approach. In Chapter Eight we will make some further comments concerning the source of this resilience.

We now turn to the agent-naturalistic explanation of the idea of something as valuable in itself. We have seen that Kant accepts the *prima facie* intelligibility of this notion. A case in point for Kant is the good will, a will which freely elects to be governed by the Categorical Imperative provided by Reason. How can we account for the apparent intelligibility of a species of willing which is good in itself? According to our argument, we should not be able to understand such a disinterested kind of valuing which is divorced from natural valuing. And yet, clearly, we do understand it.

Our explanation for the superficial intelligibility of this notion was foreshadowed in Chapter Four. There it was explained that the 'absolute'

---

[9] See *CPrR*, p. 119 n., A 5 n.

value of good willing emerges in the context of the logic of mutual trust. Thus the 'unconditional' value of trust is seen to be a function of the fact that trusting is a practice which must be done 'on principle'. For even if on a given occasion trust may not be reciprocated, we still have a 'duty' to continue to trust others to ensure the continuance of that fundamental happiness which comes through living in trusting relationships with our fellows. In general, i.e. as seen from a long-term perspective, mutual trust and its attendant happiness will result, so long as such behaviour is the rule of our society and it is, therefore, in our interest to live by that rule. If I seem to value trusting behaviour—principled behaviour (good willing)—in and for itself (and not for the happiness that a given instance of trusting behaviour may bring) I do this simply because experience has taught me, in general, that trust begets trust and that mutual trust is productive of happiness so that I regard it as a valuable practice independently of its results in any particular case.

Would people persist in trusting behaviour if their trust were not generally reciprocated? Would we have so much as the conception of acting on the principle of trust and regarding it as *right* to do so, if there were no naturally occurring positive emotional response to such behaviour (when reciprocated) which underwrote its practice? It is, we contend, reasonable to assert that such reciprocity, and the happiness it engenders, are indeed the natural origin of the 'unconditional' moral value which Kant asserts is associated with good willing. The maintenance of mutual trust is the condition upon which the possibility of satisfying all our desires rests and we therefore have an unconditional *prudential* duty to trust one another.

This alternative explanation of the unconditional character of moral precepts constitutes an agent-naturalistic explanation because it explains the behaviour in question by combining a natural explanation (referring to naturally occurring motives like the desire for happiness) with a rational explanation which involves the agent's powers to act rationally (referring to its understanding of the situation). Thus, on the one hand, the agent desires happiness (this is *why* the agent trusts others — trusting relationships are happy relationships and it is naturally motivated by its desires to seek happiness). And, on the other hand, the agent understands (either implicitly—through accumulated experience of how its happiness depends on being in a trusting relationship with other people—or explicitly—through a conscious appreciation of the fundamental interdependence of human agents) the unconditional validity of the prudential principle 'trust begets trust' and this *understanding* explains *how* it is that the agent is able to bring itself to act 'on principle' where an explicit 'desire' to trust others may be lacking.

The contrast between this agent-naturalistic explanation and Hume's naturalistic explanation of unconditional or dutiful behaviour is worth noting. For Hume, any apparent instance of an action which is performed solely out of a sense of duty will prove to have, on closer examination, a natural motive which is the real cause of this behaviour:

> But may not the sense of morality or duty produce an action, without any other motive? I answer, It may: But this is no objection to the present doctrine. When any virtuous motive or principle is common in human nature, a person, who feels his heart devoid of that motive, may hate himself upon that account, and may perform the action without the motive, from a certain sense of duty, in order to acquire by practice, that virtuous principle, or at least, to disguise to himself, as much as possible, his want of it.[10]

Clearly it is the man's self-hatred that motivates his action, not an understanding of the unconditional prudential validity of the principle concerned. His actions, in other words, do not flow from his understanding but from his desires.

To sum up: the agent-naturalist acts virtuously, not from desire (as in the case of the naturalist) nor out of a sense of duty (as is the case with the moralist) but out of the recognition (implicit or explicit) that such a way of behaving is the best policy for a finite being who needs to trust and be trusted by others if it is to be happy. The agent then treats this way of behaving as unconditionally good *relative to its finite status*. Any finite agent, just because it is finite, is inclined to lead its life in terms of the short-term pursuit of the desires it is feeling at the moment. And its understanding—its capacity for prudent behaviour—is limited by this fact. This is why the acceptance of moral rules (rules which are to be treated as unconditional) is no more than an act of prudence on the part of the agent-naturalist.[11] It is the only sane course of action once it is

---

[10] *A Treatise on Human Nature,* Translated by L.A. Selby-Bigge, Oxford University Press, Oxford, 1888, p. 479.

[11] See *Ethics*, pp. 252-253, V Proposition X Note: "The best we can do, therefore, so long as we do not possess a perfect knowledge of our emotions, is to frame a system of right conduct, or fixed practical precepts, to commit it to memory, and to apply it forthwith to the particular circumstances which now and again meet us in life, so that our imagination may become fully imbued therewith, and that it may be always ready to our

understood that moral rules have the unconditional status which they have because they promote behaviour which constitutes the precondition for the happiness of interdependent finite agents. It is for this reason that acts done out of a good will (moral acts) are the only acts which are unconditionally good: they create the conditions under which, alone, human agents can flourish and thus be happy.[12]

The Teleology of Reason.

Kant's second piece of *prima facie* evidence in support of morality is presented as an argument stemming from a teleological premise:

> In the natural constitution of an organized being, i.e., one suitably adapted to life, we assume as an axiom that no organ will be found for any purpose which is not the fittest and best adapted to that purpose. Now if its preservation, its welfare—in a word, its happiness—were the real end of nature in a being having reason and will, then nature would have hit upon a very poor arrangement in appointing the reason of the creature to be the executor of this purpose. (*FMM*, p. 56, AB 4)

A will directed by Instinct, he declares in the same passage, would have done a better job if happiness were the sole purpose of our being. Yet it remains a fact that Reason can control the will: "But reason is given to us as a practical faculty, i.e., one which is meant to have an influence on the will."[13] Therefore, since reason is so poor at securing happiness for us, why is it capable of influencing our conduct? The obvious answer, given the teleological premise, is that it is not related to the will in order to make us happy, but rather for "another and far more worthy purpose of...existence."[14]

What is this purpose? Since reasoning is an uncertain means of influencing our will where we are aiming at being happy, "reason's proper function must be to produce a will good in itself and not one good

---

hand."

[12] It is worth noting that the agent-naturalist does not regard religion, in so far as it is characterized as a body of doctrine which lays down unconditional rules for our behaviour, as anything more or less than a sober response to the finite character of human agency. Religion (like morality) serves to remind us of what we can—occasionally, in our more Spinozistic moments—recognize on our own, viz. that as finite, we need all the help we can get if we are to flourish.

[13] *FMM*, p. 58, BA 7
[14] *FMM.*, p. 57, BA 6.

merely as a means."[15] If there were a way of behaving influenced by our reasoning which, simply in virtue of according with reason's dictates thereby brought into being a value of a singular kind, i.e. a moral value, then this would explain why "reason is given to us as a practical faculty."[16] The proper function of reason could then be seen in its being a necessary condition underlying the possibility of bringing moral value into being. As creatures of instinct we are enabled to pursue happiness; as rational we are (uniquely) enabled to create and pursue moral goodness in the form of a good will. The point of reason's being practical, its having an influence on the will, is not that we might thereby be happy, but rather that we might thereby be good and we can achieve this simply by willing in accordance with reason's practically valid dictates.

Kant's argument rests on an empirical contention, viz. that reason "with its weak insight"[17] is, in fact, unable to "think out for itself a plan of happiness and the means of attaining it."[18] he declares that

> the more a cultivated reason deliberately devotes itself to the enjoyment of life and happiness, the more the man falls short of *true* contentment. (*FMM*, p. 57, AB 5, our italics.)

Now Aristotle and Spinoza would disagree with Kant here insofar as he is stating an empirical fact about the relationship between reason and happiness. But the phrase *"true* contentment" contaminates the *empirical* character of this dispute. Kant's contention turns out, after all, to rest on the claim that however happy practically wise people might find themselves through the exercise of reason over the conduct of their life, this could not constitute *true* contentment or *true*

---

[15] *FMM*, p. 58, BA 7.

[16] *loc.cit.* Were it not for the solemn, almost mystical character of the conclusion (we have a natural faculty whose ultimate purpose is to create moral value), its divergence from the expected conclusion would be quite amusing. The expected conclusion is that although reason is less than perfect in respect of sniffing out a happy life for us, it is perfectly suited as a guide to happiness for a finite being living in a complex world. Reason forms hypotheses on the basis of past experience (and the feelings that these experiences evoked) as to what course of action will maximize our happiness and—given the limited nature of its 'data-base'—it always points us in the 'right' direction. Thus reason *is* "the most appropriate [organ] to that end [given our finite condition] and best fitted for it" and therefore there is no *prima facie* need to supply it with an additional end which will somehow make teleological sense of its existence.

[17] *FMM*, p. 57 BA 5.

[18] *loc.cit.*

satisfaction. But why not? The answer lies with Kant's declaration:

> Reason is not, however, competent to guide the will safely with regard to its objects and the satisfaction of all our needs. (*FMM*, p. 57, AB 6-7)

And, of course, an Aristotle or a Spinoza could hardly dispute this contention. They might well disagree with Kant that instinct would be *better* at securing immediate happiness than reasoning, but the view that either could guide the will safely, guide the will *with certainty*,[19] in its pursuit of happiness could not be defended in the nature of the case. Thus instinct is reliable for a species as a whole because it works in most cases but a given individual is less secure in following it. And, when we behave rationally, we must wait upon experience to see whether the means, which we have reasoned will bring happiness, actually will secure it for us. We can know with certainty (in so far as our memories are faithful) that a given line of behaviour has, in the past, resulted in happiness. However, we cannot be certain that it will continue to do so in the future. The safety of acting in accordance with the course provided by our reasoned reflection on experience is not total. For a finite being, trusting appraised experience is (in proportion to the extent of the experience and the depth of the appraisal) only more or less secure and thus only more or less a source of confidence that we are on the right track in our pursuit of happiness.

Spinoza would therefore say that the solution to the problem of *securing* happiness cannot lie in finding some power in us—reason—which is not bound by finitude and which can, therefore, supply us with a certain means to happiness. Rather the solution lies in recognizing that our pursuit of happiness and our intellectual inquiry into what is the wise thing to do to secure it can be only more or less successful. Its wisdom will always be relative to our experience and the depth of critical appraisal we apply to it. Thus when Spinoza says, "By *good* I mean that which we certainly know to be useful to us",[20] what he means by "certainly know" is: "know in so far as our experience has thus far taught us." And this involves a continual process of learning from experience what is truly useful. In general, as our experience grows, we come to an

---

[19] This is Abbott's translation of *sicher* which Beck (in the just-quoted passage) translates as "safely" (*Kant's Critique of Practical Reason and Other Works on the Theory of Ethics*, translated by Thomas Kingsmill Abbott, Longmans, London, 1927). It seems to be Kant's intention that the will be secure in its direction and from an intellectual point of view this amounts to being certain.

[20] *Ethics*, p. 190, IV Definition 1.

understanding of our nature as finite agents and come to recognize our essential relationship to a world of other agents with whom we either must act in reciprocal harmony or be overwhelmed.

In Chapter Four, Desire (as the spokesperson for the view that morality is, at bottom, prudence) points out to Conscience that morality as a form of life is a Machiavellian device aimed at keeping human beings on the straight and narrow path. The assumption is that, if they were not coerced by morality, they would immediately tend towards the pursuit of short-term goals and would ultimately suffer as a consequence. But this assumption is disputable. To the degree that we rightly understand the essential reciprocity of our relationship with other agents, we do not need an absolute moral law to drag us out of a narrow, self-centred, prudential view. It is enough to understand that

> human power is extremely limited, and is infinitely surpassed by the power of external causes; we have not, therefore, an absolute power of shaping to our use those things which are without us. (*Ethics*, p. 242, IV Appendix XXXII)

If we remember this, a narrow self-centred view is just not possible. Prudence cannot then be exercised solely in respect to our own activities. It lies instead in seeing to it that we act in ever-increasing harmony with the entire world of other agents, human and otherwise. As Spinoza says,

> Nevertheless, we shall bear with an equal mind all that happens to us in contravention to the claims of our own advantage, so long as we are conscious that we have done our duty, and that the power which we possess is not sufficient to enable us to protect ourselves completely; remembering that we are a part of universal nature, and that we follow her order. If we have a clear and distinct understanding of this, that part of our nature which is defined by intelligence, in other words the better part of ourselves, will assuredly acquiesce in what befalls us, and in such acquiescence will endeavour to persist. For, in so far as we are intelligent beings, we cannot desire anything save that which is necessary, nor yield absolute acquiescence to anything, save to that which is true: wherefore, in so far as we have a right understanding of these things, the endeavour of the better part of ourselves is in harmony with the order of nature as a whole. (*Ethics,* p. 242-243, IV Appendix XXXII)

Kant's contrary claim that using reason to secure happiness is a misuse of reason (just because reason cannot direct us to happiness with certainty) is according to Spinoza, a misconstrual of the nature of reasoning. To see Kant's mistake let us consider his own view of what reasoning consists in:

> Reason, considered as the faculty of a certain logical form of knowledge, is the faculty of inferring, i.e. judging mediately (by the subsumption of the condition of a possible judgment under the condition of a given judgment). (*CPR*, p. 320, A 330 B 386, cf. p. 534-535, A 646 B 674)

Reasoning always involves following the rule of subsumption or class-inclusion.[21] Since this rule is quite intuitive, reasoning proceeds 'automatically': we see 'straightway' how the conclusion necessarily follows from the premises.

When reasoning operates with terms which are well defined it delivers certain conclusions. When we understand clearly what, for example, men are and what mortality is and, when we are told that a certain individual—Socrates—is a man, then we see, with certainty, that Socrates is mortal. However, the truth of the conclusion is not a function of the intuitive certainty we have that the rules for deriving the conclusion have been followed correctly (that we have here recognized a case of class-inclusion). The truth of the conclusion is a function of the truth of the premises. If the premises are true then the conclusion derived from them will also be true.

So reasoning, as it operates in proceeding from premises to conclusion, cannot be construed as an instrument which provides us with certain truths simply in virtue of its employment as our means of seeing 'straightway' the implicative relationship between the premises and the conclusion. To repeat: the certainty which reasoning provides us with is the certainty that, if the premises are true, then so is the conclusion.

Thus when Kant says that reasoning is not competent to direct the will with certainty he cannot be complaining about some lack in our capacity to reason. For, on Kant's own view, reason's competence in moving from premises to conclusion is not really in question. He can, therefore, only be pointing out that the premises upon which we might reason out a plan of action in order to secure "the satisfaction of all our needs",[22] are bound to be insufficient. Our experience—the source of our

---

[21] See note 28 to Chapter Two.
[22] *FMM*, p. 57, BA 7.

premises—is limited but the reasoning which is based on such premises is not thereby shorn of its power to let us see *with certainty* what the implications of our past experience are, given the premises upon which we are reasoning. Using reason we *can* know with certainty that *if* the future is like the past, *then* doing x will bring satisfaction, since, in the past, it has done so.

Reason then, on Kant's own understanding of it, cannot be regarded as a faculty which suffers inherently from "weak insight".[23] Its 'weakness' lies rather in the finite range of past experience upon which Reason must rely to project what we should do to secure our future happiness. Thus the complaint that we, in our finitude, fail to find 'true contentment' or 'true satisfaction' through standard prudential reasoning[24] should not have driven Kant to suppose that there was some special employment of Reason which would yield a true (superior) contentment as a kind of compensation for Reason's inadequacy in the sphere of prudence. In short, he did not have to suppose that, on account of its incapacity with respect to prudence,

> reason ... is capable only of a contentment of its own kind, i.e., one that springs from the attainment of a purpose, which in turn is determined by reason. (*FMM*, p. 58, AB 7-8)

What purpose or end is it that Kant supposes reason could determine by itself (and thus come into the possession of its own peculiar kind of contentment)? Reason functions as that faculty which 'sees' the implications which link premises to conclusions. Reason follows these implications or rules when it draws conclusions from premises. Suppose then that there were a peculiar contentment to be gained from the practice of rule-following itself, a satisfaction to be gained from acting in accordance with a rule simply for the the sake of acting in accordance with a rule. If this were so, then it would follow that the consequences of acting in accordance with the rule would be irrelevant to the contentment to be gained from the practice of rule following for its own sake. Acting in this way would then yield a satisfaction or contentment of its own proper kind, quite independently of empirical considerations (e.g. happiness). This would 'explain', at least teleologically, Reason's capacity to influence the will. The means—

---

[23] *FMM*., p. 57, BA 5.
[24] We 'fail' because we lack complete knowledge of the ways of the world as they relate to the satisfaction of all our wants.

reasoning or rule-following—would then be seen to be perfectly adapted to the end—the satisfaction[25] of simply following rules = willing rationally.

That such a satisfaction exists is undeniable. People delight, or at the very least, see considerable value, in acting on principle simply for the sake of being principled (being a rule-follower, being rational). On the other hand, however, the legitimacy of taking unrestrained delight in this kind of behaviour and the contention that this delight signals an unconditionally valuable way of behaving, is very much open to dispute.[26] As Montaigne puts it:

> Now the laws maintain their credit, not because they are just, but because they are laws. This is the mystical basis of their authority; they have no other. And this serves them well. They are often made by fools, and more often by men who, out of hatred for equality, are lacking in equity, but always by men: vain and unstable creatures. There is nothing so grossly and widely nor so ordinarily faulty as the laws. Whoever obeys them because they are just [i.e. legal] is not, as he should be, obeying them for a just reason.[27]

The "mystical basis" of moral value is the idea that rule-following, *being* rational, is good in itself. In truth, it is not good in itself: its value is conditioned resting on the fact that a moral rule (e.g. Do not lie), derived from the experience of many, has been generally found to be a reliable means of securing happiness, contentment, peace of mind or whatever we choose to call the resulting satisfaction. However, the actual value of following such a rule blindly, following it simply because it is

---

[25] In accordance with Kant's own usage this does not entail that, because it results in a satisfaction, the desire to follow rules is just another inclination. The satisfaction or contentment here would be what Kant himself calls a "negative satisfaction" (*CPrR*, p. 222, A 213)—a genuine experience yet one without any positive character; not an experience which is the result of gaining a particular and clearly defined object. Rather it comes with being "conscious of needing nothing" (*CPrR*, p. 221, A 212), i.e. of not being bound by inclination and therefore being free to be ruled by reason alone.

[26] There is certainly a special value which we attach to acting on principle, but at the same time, we consider its value to be conditioned by the content of the principle that is acted upon. Hume delights in making this point. See *A Treatise of Human Nature*, translated by L.A. Selby-Bigge, Oxford University Press, Oxford, 1888, pp. 477-501.

[27] *Essays*, Translated by J. M. Cohen, Penguin, Middlesex, 1958. p. 353.

deemed right to follow such rules, lies with the power that an accepted general rule (a 'moral' rule) has to make us stop and think about what we should do. Such a 'moral' pause allows our judgmental feelings to play their role in guiding our behaviour wisely, i.e. with due reference to our past experience.

We are now in a position to conclude the agent-naturalistic explanation of how rational behaviour comes to be invested with a special 'value', a value which must be presented as unconditional if it is to convince us that we have an obligation to realize it in our behaviour. If moral maxims were presented simply as the counsels of prudence and their only sanction was the weight of the collective experience of the culture, acceptance of their counsel and an appreciation of their wisdom would be far from easy to attain. It would in fact have to wait upon the development of a capacity to appreciate wisdom, which would be wisdom itself.[28] Moral maxims, seen in this way, have their value not as fundamental guides to behaviour, valid prior to and independent of experience, but as products of experience, as rules we have developed for our own use. So for moral maxims to influence behaviour in advance of wisdom (a quality of mind which can only be accumulated *via* long experience) they must be presented as if they—the maxims of prudence—were not simply generally applicable, but instead as if they were universally applicable, as if they were a set of principles which always worked and therefore should always be obeyed.

For a finite agent there can be no absolutely unconditional rules. Its finite experience yields only conditional rules, rules conditioned by what the agent has thus far learned (from its own experience and that of others) about the best ways to achieve happiness. Thus for the agent-naturalist, the delights of following the dictates of Reason are not to be found in the 'peculiar' satisfaction of rule-following for its own sake, but rather in recognizing that reason is our best guide in an uncertain world.

Respect for the Moral Law

A third piece of *prima facie* empirical evidence for the existence of morality as a form of life is the feeling of respect. Respect for the moral law is a natural effect on feeling of the intellect's recognition of the universal validity of this law. When people act solely out of their

---

[28] One of the mildly amusing things about getting older is the gradual realization that all the clichés about life and living (the natural locus of our collective wisdom) are, in fact, true.

recognition of the validity of the moral law, it is their feeling of respect for the moral law that provides the incentive for their behaviour. However, this incentive to the will is not, according to Kant, a natural feeling, in the sense of being

> received through any [outer] influence but is self-wrought by a rational concept; thus it differs specifically from all feelings of the former kind which may be referred to inclination or fear. What I recognize directly as a law for myself I recognize with respect, which means merely the consciousness of the submission of my will to a law without the intervention of other influences on my mind. The direct determination of the will by the law and the consciousness of this determination is respect;[29] thus respect can be regarded as the effect of the law on the subject and not as the cause of the law. (*FMM*, p. 62n, AB 16n.)

From this we can appreciate that respect for the moral law, although not a naturally occurring feeling, is still a genuine feeling. Furthermore, it constitutes, for Kant, a crucial part of what we have called the shadow model of moral causality, so crucial that, without it, the model could not be put into practical effect. We now want to examine the precise nature of this phenomenon and consider whether it is amenable to an agent-naturalistic explanation.

We know that Kant regards moral value as an absolute or unconditional value, a value which is independent of any object to be gained as a consequence of action. There cannot be anything 'in it' for us when we act morally. Therefore the *motivation* provided by the feeling of respect must constitute a unique form of motivation. Kant is very careful on this point:

> What is essential in the moral worth of actions is that the moral law should directly determine the will. If the determination of the will occurs in accordance with the moral law *but only by means of a feeling of any kind*

---

[29] Abbott and Beck both translate *Achtung* as "respect", while Paton (H. J. Paton, *The Moral Law*, Hutchinson University Library, London, 1948) alone uses "reverence". We prefer "respect", for reasons that will become clearer as the argument proceeds. The connotations of "reverence" indicate that the moral law is absolute and sacrosanct and thus prejudge its status. "Respect", on the other hand, is a term which can be applied to our attitude towards principled behaviour which is not confined to behaviour actuated by moral (universally valid) laws. For example, we would respect (but not 'reverence') an athlete's determination to stick to the rules of a training programme.

> *whatsoever* [our italics], which must be presupposed in order that the law may become a determining ground of the will, and if the action thus occurs not for the sake of the law, it has legality but not morality. Now, if by an incentive (*elater animi*) we understand a subjective determining ground of a will whose reason does not by its nature necessarily conform to the objective law, it follows ... that the [moral] incentive of the human will (and that of every created rational being) can never be anything other than the moral law; and ... that the objective determining ground must at the same time be the exclusive and subjectively sufficient determining ground of action if the latter is to fulfil not merely the letter of the law but also its spirit. (*CPrR*, p. 180, A 126-127)

In this paragraph Kant is quite clear about the non-moral status of an action brought about by "a feeling of any kind whatsoever". So if respect is a feeling, it must not function as the *cause* of our moral behaviour—it must not move us to act. What sort of feeling is it then that registers for us the inciting character of the moral law (presents it in a positive light) without thereby causing us to act in accordance with it?

Kant introduces the complex phenomenology of this feeling of respect in the following way (continuing from the above quotation):

> Any further motives which would make it possible for us to dispense with that of moral law must not be sought, for they would only produce hypocrisy without any substance. Even to let other motives (such as those toward certain advantages) co-operate with the moral law is risky. Therefore, for the purpose of giving the moral law influence on the will, nothing remains but to determine carefully in what way the moral law becomes an incentive and, since the moral law is such an incentive, to see what happens to the human faculty of desire as a consequence of this determining ground. (*CPrR*, p. 180, A 127-128.)

In turning to the details of its role as an incentive, Kant shows that at first the moral law works—affects the human faculty of desire—negatively by "rejecting [sensuous impulses] ... and checking all inclinations so far as they could be antagonistic to the law."[30] And the result of this checking is also a feeling:

> For all inclination and every sensuous impulse is based on feeling, and the negative effect on feeling (through the check on the inclinations) is itself feeling. (*CPrR*, p.181, A 128-129.)

---

[30] *CPrR*, p. 181, A 128.

But there is also a positive aspect to the incentive provided by the moral law:

> Since this law, however, is in itself positive, being the form of an intellectual causality, i.e., the form of freedom, it is at the same time an object of respect, since, in conflict with its subjective antagonists (our inclinations), it weakens self-conceit. And as striking down, i.e., humiliating, self-conceit, it is an object of the greatest respect and thus the ground of a positive feeling which is not of empirical origin. This feeling, then, is one which can be known *a priori*. Respect for the moral law, therefore, is a feeling produced by an intellectual cause, and this feeling is the only one which we can know completely *a priori* and the necessity of which we can discern. (*CPrR*, p. 181-182, A 130.)

Experience certainly agrees with Kant in this. We are, indeed, chastened by the recognition of the rightness of a maxim which is based on sound reasoning and we do feel respect (a positive admiration) for the moral strength of people who choose to act solely out of regard for a principle like truth-telling. But the phenomenology of respect is not confined to this. Respect for the moral law is, in origin, a respect for the wise judgment this law reflects. Thus we have a natural respect for people who take upon themselves the responsibility for judging autonomously even where this judgment contravenes a moral law. Thus our natural respect for people increases when, for example, they judge that in a particular set of circumstances the telling of a lie is more appropriate than acting out of blind respect for a moral maxim ('Never tell a lie'). This is because we recognize that moral maxims are, after all, only *in general* the best way to behave if we are to flourish as agents.

Thus our overall respect for the judgment of people will have two aspects. The first is based on our admiration for their willingess to take on the responsibility for their own behaviour. This amounts to a respect for their willingness to trust their own judgment and stand by it. The second is directed towards the wisdom that is evident in the new maxim which they have adopted in the circumstances. (It might amount to the recognition that the community's interests (the happiness of its members) will be better served by this action than by an action governed strictly by the moral law.) Now on the *a priori* model of the origins of the feeling of respect, our respect should rest solely on our recognition of the rightness of the particular maxim, based ultimately on its analytic authority. Why then does the natural feeling of respect have two aspects?

Spinoza has an explanation for this difference. Our feeling of respect has these two aspects because (in the first place) it is directed much more to the *degree* of wisdom manifested in the individual agent's response to its circumstances. It is a recognition of the *wisdom* of the response considered impartially but it is also a recognition of it as a case of a person deliberately formulating a judgment and then acting upon it. Since the wisdom of our judgments is, by definition, never complete or certain, our respect for a given judgment will always be partially directed towards the active deliberation of the people concerned. Our respect will thus be a function of our recognition of the thoroughness of their consideration of the problem confronting them. Their willingness to act and their understanding (the thinking that informs their willingness) are never separate and our respect is thus directed to these two interrelated aspects of the *increased activity* of such agents. In more familiar terms, what we respect is the contribution agents themselves make to increasing their ability to cope wisely with the circumstances in which they find themselves.

But this central characteristic of an agent-naturalistic conception of morality, viz. taking upon oneself the responsibility for one's actions through the conscious exercise of one's judgment, is effectively missing in the Kantian scheme of morality. On Kant's view, respect for the maxim in question precludes our *taking* responsibility for acting in accordance with it. Moral respect is incited in us owing to the fact that the maxim in question is perceived as a law 'necessary in itself' and thus not a matter upon which there is any room for us to exercise our judgment with regard to its validity in a given set of circumstances. We could not act solely out of respect for the law (morally) if the law were regarded simply as a pragmatically derived maxim which had only general (as opposed to universal) validity. Therefore it is *obedience*, incited by respect for the law, rather than *responsibility*, which is the operative term for Kant so far as moral behaviour is concerned. Thus in his view the value of our actions is not a matter of how we *respond* to our circumstances, but whether we are willing to *obey* the moral maxim which is supposed to be the valid guide for us under these circumstances.

Indeed the logic of taking responsibility for one's actions, on the basis of having made a conscious judgment of what would be the best thing to do in a given set of circumstances, has no place in the moral form of life as Kant describes it. For example, responsibility cannot be accepted or imputed to another with any certainty within the Kantian system. Kant's reasons for believing this to be the case are apparent in the following passage:

> The real morality of actions, their merit or guilt, even that of our own conduct ... remains entirely hidden from us. Our imputations can refer only to the empirical character. How much of this character is ascribable to the pure effect of freedom, how much to mere nature, that is, to faults of temperament for which there is no responsibility, or to its happy constitution (*merito fortunae*), can never be determined; and upon it therefore no perfectly just judgments can be passed. (*CPR*, p. 475n, A 55ln B 579n.)

In any given instance, the true cause of a person's action is something that can never be determined. How strange it is that we can never, according to Kant's theory, judge ourselves or others to be responsible—to any degree at all—for the actions we perform. For in practice we do it constantly and apparently to some effect. Of course we do so with the full awareness that our judgments are the judgments of finite beings and that therefore our verdicts are always implicitly qualified with the phrase 'more or less'. In keeping with this realization we judge ourselves to be more responsible—more willing to accept a greater imputation of responsibility for a given action—the more we are conscious of having given the matter due consideration.[31] Furthermore, how strange it is that, in the *Kantian* system, where 'ought' implies 'can' and 'can' presupposes freedom, no responsibility can be imputed to individuals for their actions.

---

[31] We have, then, no fundamental reason to question the legitimacy of such 'more or less' imputations of responsibility. Exact attributions of responsibility—"perfectly just judgments" (*CPrR*, p. 475n, A 55ln B 759n)—are not appropriate to finite agents whose control over their agency is limited and variable. But rough imputations are perfectly legitimate. People can always say in their own case to what extent they felt themselves to be in control of their actions and therefore to what extent they are willing to take responsibility for what happens as a result (i.e. accept, or refuse to accept, praise or blame). Furthermore, people are well aware of whether the degree to which they were in control of their behaviour was in accord with the accepted standard for controlling oneself which is recognized by society at large. This standard defines what I mean by 'ought' when I say that people ought (i.e. have a 'duty') to behave responsibly. They ought to behave in this way, not in the categorical sense that it is their moral duty to do so, but in the hypothetical sense that they ought so to behave if they want to enjoy the respect of their fellows, if they want to be accepted as *human* agents, beings who have the capacity to be more or less in control of their behaviour.

Freedom, on Kant's understanding of it, is a notion which involves the idea of our possessing a capacity for absolute control over our behaviour. On this view, because we possess this absolute capacity to control our actions, we have therefore an absolute obligation to behave morally, an obligation which, in the context of absolute free choice, becomes an absolute responsibility. Nothing less then this 'standard' of behaviour will satisfy the logic of the demand contained in the categorical imperative.

Now the agent-naturalistic interpretation of 'ought' (implies 'can') only presupposes that the agent's capacity to control its behaviour should be in line with the general human capacity to act in accordance with one's judgment. The agent is only expected to show that degree of control over its behaviour that most people on most occasions can be expected to exhibit. The agent-naturalistic 'ought' derives its normative force from the notion of a realizable standard and it is from *this* idea that we get our quite natural sense of 'ought' implies 'can' and our understanding of what responsible behaviour amounts to.

This raises an interesting point. To regard yourself as an exceptional case, to believe that you cannot be expected to behave responsibly, is to define yourself as incapable of realizing a standard of behaviour which is, by definition, realizable by a normal person. And in quite an obvious fashion such a self-assessment is self-contradictory since if you are abnormal in the sense required, you would be incapable of recognizing this fact about yourself. This is why, on an agent-naturalistic interpretation of morality, I cannot treat myself as an exception to the fact (not the rule) that human beings can behave responsibly. I can only be an exceptional case where *others*[32] judge that my capacity to respond normally is impaired and that I am therefore not responsible for my actions.

In other words, agent-naturalistic morality is like Kantian morality in that it finds something self-contradictory in an agent acting as if it were the exception to the rule. But when such behaviour occurs, the agent-naturalist does not condemn the person in question for being immoral as the Kantian must. Instead the agent-naturalist regards that person as one who lacks judgment (either in the sense that his or her judgment is impaired or in the less severe sense of simply not having developed a

---

[32] It is quite clear at this point that morality—in agent-naturalistic terms: behaving well—is not something entirely self-wrought, not a matter of personal achievement alone. To behave well requires judgment and wisdom and to cultivate these we need the help of others. What counts as responsible behaviour is a matter for communal assessment.

sufficiently normal sense of responsibility, one that precludes making an exception of oneself).

We have argued that there is a sound agent-naturalistic account of respect which redirects this feeling towards our capacity to behave responsibly. It is the exercise of this capacity which naturally elicits respect from us and we should therefore be chary of feeling that blind respect which, Kant maintains, is the necessary concomitant of our recognition of the 'universal' practical validity of the moral law. For, as we have intimated, the 'blindness' of this respect is a function of the agent's mistakenly regarding the moral maxim as universally valid (not just a good general rule) and therefore abjuring any right to question (take the responsibility for) the law's application to the agent's behaviour in a given set of circumstances. The notoriety of Kant's Essay, 'On A Supposed Right To Lie From Altruistic Motives', is a function of our reaction to the irresponsibility of blindly following the moral law, whatever the circumstances may be.[33]

Something further needs to be said about the existence of that complex phenomenology that characterizes the Kantian notion of respect. This is necessary because people do experience this feeling of blind, unquestioning respect and, on the basis of this, are inclined to accept the reality of the moral form of life:

> In the boundless esteem for the pure moral law, removed from all advantage, as practical reason presents it to us for obedience, whose voice makes even the boldest sinner tremble and forces him to hide himself from it, there is something so singular that we cannot wonder at finding this influence of a merely intellectual idea on feeling to be inexplicable to speculative reason, and at having to be satisfied with being able to see *a priori* that such a feeling is inseparably bound with the idea of the

---

[33] 'On A Supposed Right To Tell A Lie From Altruistic Motives', included in *CPrR*, pp. 346-350. The question addressed by Kant is whether it is right to tell a lie to save a person's life, whether it would be right to say to an intending murderer at your door that his intended victim is not at home (when he or she in fact is at home). As far as Kant is concerned there are no mitigating circumstances that could give a person the right to tell a lie: "To be truthful (honest) in all declarations, therefore, is a sacred and absolutely commanding decree of reason, limited by no expediency" (p. 348). More significantly and detrimentally, this rules out considering how other people expect one to behave. Does the intended victim expect you to tell the truth (and therefore slip out the back door, as suggested)? Does the intending murderer expect you to tell the truth—and expect his victim in turn to expect that you will, and therefore run round to the back door etc.?

moral law in every finite rational being. (*CPrR*, p. 187, A 141-142.)

Given that this boundless esteem is experienced, how can it be explained on the agent-naturalistic view? One possible explanation runs as follows: the reverence with which a finite rational being regards the moral law has its origins in two related factors. The first is our tendency to promote generally sound practical maxims to the status of universally valid practical laws. This tendency is rooted in the second factor, viz. an understandable desire on the part of finite agents for fail-safe maxims which, if followed, will relieve them of the necessity of justifying their actions in terms of their utilitarian consequences. Thus if I tell the truth out of respect for the universal practical validity of the truth-telling maxim and this action on my part has disastrous consequences (in utilitarian terms), the moral value of my act remains unaffected. No wonder then that I respect the moral law: it allows for a method of behaving that has a guaranteed value independently of utilitarian standards of value.

The attractions of moral behaviour are therefore obvious. Such behaviour allows us to create value in our lives, whatever the contingencies of life may be in terms of the utilitarian results of our behaviour (in terms of our own and other people's happiness). However, if we are to enjoy this advantage, we must be able to promote the good general rules of conduct derived from experience to the status of universally valid maxims. And since the move from 'usually' to 'always' is invalid (however tempting) its invalidity must in some way be masked. How does this happen?

If a maxim is to be recognized as universally valid it would help if the maxim were couched in terms which gave it the appearance of being true by definition (though, of course, not too obviously so). Thus suppose I begin with the empirical maxim 'Honesty is the best policy' (meaning: 'In general, people have found more happiness by being honest with each other than by being deceitful'). Now I want to make this true by definition. How is this to be achieved? It could be done by making the maxim analytic with reference to the character of the interior life of a person. This could be done by stipulating that, 'in fact', satisfactions gained through deceit are not actually satisfying to the one who experiences them. We would have to declare that, 'as a matter of fact', only those satisfactions which result from behaviour which follows the rule of honesty are experienced as satisfying and anyone who experiences things differently would simply fall outside this 'factual' definition of what human beings are like.Thus any experience that we might have of finding the fruits of deceit satisfying would have to be denied all authority.

But now a daunting question must be answered: do I have the power to render a satisfaction unsatisfying through the moral 'knowledge' that it is not? (E.g. the 'knowledge' that 'Any satisfaction brought about through deceit will be experienced as unsatisfying', this being the corollary of the practical law: 'Only honest dealings with others can bring us satisfaction').

It is probably fair to say that this moral knowledge would not have this effect if I were aware of the definitional character of the process whereby it was established as a 'fact'. The definitional basis of such knowledge must somehow be disguised so that I can believe the maxim to be a matter of empirical fact, a fact which turns on the nature of human beings as finite rational creatures. I must believe that such moral knowledge is really knowledge about the nature of human beings as they are. If I believe this, then I can come to regard any 'inappropriate' feelings which I may experience as illusory in character. I can then dismiss their evident relish—their apparent capacity to satisfy—as a snare and a delusion. (I might even imagine someone else, the Devil perhaps, as responsible for making me feel these false satisfactions.) Thus my belief in the moral law as a universally valid injunction which necessarily has application to me as a rational creature will produce feelings which will protect me against inappropriately getting any satisfaction out of even a harmless lie.[34] Any such satisfaction is not a true satisfaction and is quite inferior to the real value of life.

It is here that we see the most potent feature of language (in this case in the context of the language game of morality)—its power to edit our experience so that it will support our beliefs. Because of this feature, our respect, in the form of an utter reverence for the moral law, will receive 'direct' support from our experience in that any recalcitrant experience will be dismissed as inferior if not completely illusory. This explains the

---

[34] Cf. "This idea of personality awakens respect; it places before our eyes the sublimity of our own nature (in its [higher] vocation), while it shows us at the same time the unsuitability of our conduct to it, thus striking down our self-conceit. This is naturally and easily observed by the most common human reason. Has not every even fairly honest man sometimes found that he desists from an otherwise harmless lie which would extricate him from a vexing affair or which would even be useful to a beloved and deserving friend simply in order not to have to contemn himself secretly in his own eyes?" *CPrR*, p. 194, A 156-157.

negative aspect of respect, its power to cast down and humiliate our feelings when they do not agree with the moral law.[35] Respect for the moral law can effectively discount our natural feelings as trustworthy guides to our behaviour (if we 'want'[36] to behave morally). This is indicative of the unconditional power which the moral law wields to edit our experience of value and thus provides phenomenological support for the reality of the moral form of life. However there is still the question of actually obeying this moral law which elicits our respect, the question of acting through the incentive of respect for the moral law. If feeling respect is to promote being good (i.e. if it is to incite us to will solely out of respect for the universal validity of the moral law) then there is a *prima facie* case for supposing that being good must, in some sense of the word, be a *satisfying* experience. Otherwise, why should the feeling of respect incite us to act? What then is 'satisfying' about being good if this satisfaction is not to be founded on a utilitarian value (the feeling of happiness) which is brought about by being good? To answer this question we now turn to Kant's discussion of self-contentment.

Self-Contentment

A fourth piece of *prima facie* evidence for morality is the existence of the feeling of self-contentment. This is an important piece of evidence for Kant since his careful definition of the phenomenological quality of this feeling serves, in his view, to provide the "solution of the antinomy of pure practical reason".[37] The antinomy raises the following difficulty:

happiness and morality are two specifically different elements of the highest good and therefore their combination cannot be known analytically (as if a person who sought his happiness found himself virtuous

---

[35] We must agree with Kant that anything which humiliates self-conceit has considerable value. Self-conceit is the result of following a self-centred perspective and our chief problem as human beings living with others is to achieve a less self-centred perspective. Since our perspective will always be more or less self-centred (our finitude ensures this and we are perversely inclined to ignore this fact), we are advised to coax ourselves into as broad a view as possible, using the wisdom which principles such as the moral law contain. The feeling of self-conceit, or of pride, is not, then, totally destroyed. Rather we experience humiliation which, for the time being, reduces self-conceit to a more manageable level. On an agent-naturalistic interpretation, feelings such as pride, though inerradicable, can be gradually toned down as a person recognizes—not the essential wickedness of such feelings—but the lack of wisdom implicit in being ruled by them.

[36] See Desire's comment on Reason's 'wanting', p. 25 above.

[37] CPrR, p. 223, A 214.

merely through solving his problem, or one who followed virtue found himself *ipso facto* happy in the consciousness of his conduct). (*CPrR*, p. 217, A 203.)

This is Kant's statement of the problem that generates the Antinomy of Practical Reason. The highest good is the supreme motivation of the human will—the furthering of the highest good, which contains this connection in its concept, is an *a priori* necessary object of our will and is inseparably related to the moral law.[38]

The highest good is the concept which links happiness and morality. The nature of the necessity of this concept is expressed by Kant in the following passage:

For to be in need of happiness and also worthy of it and yet not to partake of it could not be in accordance with the complete volition of an omnipotent rational being, if we assume such only for the sake of the argument. (*CPrR*, p. 215, A 199)

And yet Kant maintains that, in experience, we do not find anything but a contingent relation between them. In fact, he considers that there can be no necessary (in the sense of analytic[39]) connection between virtue and happiness. Those who claim that there is—for example the Epicureans and Stoics—deny the heterogeneity of these two elements of the highest good. But, says Kant, the Analytic of the *Critique of Practical Reason* has already established that

the maxims of virtue and those of one's own happiness are wholly heterogeneous and far removed from being at one in respect to their supreme practical principle; and even though they belong to a highest good, which they jointly make possible, they strongly limit and check each other in the same subject. (*CPrR*, p. 217, A 202.)

Although these two elements are involved in the highest good, we find that in striving to be happy *and* virtuous our endeavour is at odds with itself: success on the one side removes the possibility of attaining

---

[38] CPrR, p. 218, A 205.
[39] "Two terms necessarily combined in one concept must be related as ground and consequence, and this unity must be regarded either as analytic (logical connection) according to the law of identity or as synthetic (real connection) according to the law of causality." CPrR, p. 215, A 199- 200.

success on the other. If we act out of a desire for happiness we cannot be, by definition, behaving virtuously. On the other hand virtuous behaviour is (again, by definition) simply that behaviour which we pursue without any reference to the satisfaction of our inclinations, i.e. those desires which promise happiness. In short, the logic of the moral form of life rules out the possibility of linking virtue and happiness in an analytically necessary concept of the highest good.

But if this connection cannot be thought analytically, then

> it must be thought synthetically and, more particularly, as the connection of cause and effect, for it concerns a practical good, i.e., one that is possible through action. Therefore, the desire for happiness must be the motive to maxims of virtue, or the maxim of virtue must be the efficient cause of happiness. (*CPrR*, p. 217, A 204.)

However when we examine these two cases we find that so far as the second alternative is concerned the facts cut both ways: Kant was well aware that in the opinion of the Epicureans, and the Stoics, being good made a person feel happy. Thus he notes:

> ...it must appear strange that philosophers of both ancient and modern times have been able to find happiness in very just proportion to virtue in *this* life (in the world of sense) or at least have been able to convince themselves of it. For Epicurus as well as the Stoics extolled happiness springing from the consciousness of virtuous living above everything else. (*CPrR*, p. 219, A 208.)

Kant is then forced to maintain that these philosophers had misdescribed the phenomenological character of this 'happiness' which sprang from the consciousness of virtuous living. What in fact people feel as a result of being virtuous, is not happiness but (claims Kant) an analogue of happiness:

> Do we not have a word to denote a satisfaction with existence, an analogue of happiness which necessarily accompanies the consciousness of virtue, and which does not indicate a gratification, as "happiness" does? We do, and this word is "self-contentment", which in its real meaning refers only to negative satisfaction with existence in which one is conscious of needing nothing. Freedom and the consciousness of freedom, as a capacity for following the moral law with an unyielding disposition,

is independence from inclinations, at least as motives determining (though not as affecting) our desiring; and, so far as I am conscious of freedom in obeying my moral maxims, it is the exclusive source of an unchanging contentment necessarily connected with it and resting on no particular feeling. This may be called intellectual contentment. Sensuous contentment (improperly so called) which rests on the satisfaction of inclinations, however refined they may be, can never be adequate to that which is conceived under contentment. (*CPrR*, pp. 221- 222, A 211-212)

Kant then once more describes the negative quality of this satisfaction which allows it to be a satisfaction yet not a satisfaction which is commensurable with the positive satisfaction commonly known as happiness:

Thus we can understand how the consciousness of this capacity of a pure practical reason through a deed (virtue) can produce a consciousness of mastery over inclinations and thus of independence from them and from the discontentment which always accompanies them, bringing forth a negative satisfaction with one's condition, i.e., contentment, whose source is contentment with one's own person. Freedom itself thus becomes in this indirect way capable of an enjoyment. *This cannot be called happiness*, since it does not depend upon a positive participation of feeling; nor can it be called bliss, because it does not include complete independence from inclinations and desires. It does nevertheless resemble the latter so far at least as the determination of the will which it involves can be held to be free from their influence, and thus, at least in its origin, it is analogous to the self-sufficiency which can be ascribed only to the Supreme Being. (*CPrR*, pp. 222-223, A 213-214, our italics.)

There is an American expression which aptly characterizes Kant's efforts to 'purify' the satisfaction we find in behaving morally: 'No matter how thin you slice it, it's still baloney'. Kant's problem here can be illustrated by considering those emotional states which are characterized by such expressions as 'moral fervour' and 'righteousness'. These emotional states bear eloquent testimony to the positive satisfactions available to those who regard themselves as acting 'solely' out of respect for duty. The emotional states to which these expressions refer do constitute a source of satisfaction—"a positive participation of feeling"—for many individuals. But (as the single quotation marks around the word 'solely' are meant to imply) if one is to behave morally, one cannot allow the experience of the value which acting in this way creates, to be felt in a positive fashion, to be experienced as gratifying. One cannot behave morally and positively enjoy it. That would amount to indulging oneself and therefore ceasing to act out of the pure thought of duty. Yet how is this 'indulgence' to be prevented? How can people confine their motivation to their respect for the validity of the moral law once they have experienced the happiness which springs from the "consciousness of virtuous living"? How can they help developing a 'taste for virtue'?[40]

Now as we know, Kant was well aware of the psychological pitfalls which pure moral activity must avoid if it is to maintain its purity, in particular the problem of subreption noted earlier:[41]

> But, on the other hand, there is always here an occasion for a subreption (*vitium subreptionis*) and, as it were, for an optical illusion in the self-consciousness of what one does in contradistinction to what one feels, which even the most experienced person cannot entirely avoid. The moral disposition is necessarily connected with a consciousness of the determination of the will directly by a law. Now the consciousness of a determination of the faculty of desire is always a ground for satisfaction in the resulting action; but this pleasure, this satisfaction with one's self, is not the determining ground of the action; on the contrary, the determination of the will directly by reason alone is the ground of the feeling of pleasure, and this remains a pure practical determination of the faculty of desire, not a sensuous one. Since this determination produces the same inward effect, i.e., an impulse to activity, *as does a feeling of agreeableness which is expected from the desired action*, we see that what we ourselves do may easily be looked upon as something which we merely passively feel, the moral motive being held to be a sensuous impulse, as it always occurs in so-called illusions of the senses (and here we have such an illusion of the inner sense). (*CPrR*, pp. 220-221, A 209-210, our italics.)

This is an important point and Kant emphasizes it in what immediately follows this quotation.

---

[40] See Aristotle, 'Nichomachean Ethics', translated by Sir David Ross, in *The Basic Works of Aristotle*, ed. Richard McKeon, Random House, New York, 1941, pp. 1108-1109, 1179b 14-16.

[41] See pp. 54 *ff.*, above.

It is a very sublime thing in human nature to be determined to actions directly by a pure law of reason, and even the illusion wherein the subjective element of this intellectual determinability of the will is held to be sensuous and an effect of a particular sensuous feeling [our desire for self-contentment]...*partakes of this sublimity. It is of great importance to point out this quality of our personality and to cultivate so far as possible the effect of reason on this feeling.* But we must, nevertheless, be on guard against degrading and deforming the real and authentic incentive, the law itself, by awarding spurious praise to the moral ground of determination as incentive as though it were based on feelings of particular joys, thus setting it, as it were, against a false foil; for these joys are only its consequences. (*CPrR*, p. 221, A 210-211)

In the italicized phrase in the previous quotation, Kant indicates very clearly his awareness that self-contentment is an agreeable state of mind and, as such, may constitute a natural motive for acting virtuously. However, he staunchly maintains that the feeling of self-contentment, although undeniably a feeling, is nevertheless not a positive satisfaction and therefore not commensurable with other feelings which all stem from the satisfaction of a desire. We are therefore required to experience self-contentment (value it) strictly as an analogue of happiness, as a satisfaction which is not a satisfaction in the natural sense.

Why then does Kant hold fast to this problematic notion of self-contentment, a satisfaction that is not a satisfaction? The answer is that the moral form of life he is defending requires such a notion. But why is the moral form of life so important that it requires this thoroughgoing editing of our experience? For the answer to this we must turn to Kant's discussion of Dignity.[43]

Dignity

Of all the elements which together go to make up the moral form of life, dignity is the most potent and the most difficult to explain away. According to Kant, it is through the experience of dignity that human beings become acquainted with the intrinsic value which attaches to them as beings capable of moral behaviour. Kant introduces the notion of dignity as follows:

---

[43] It will be more economical to discuss the agent-naturalistic account of self-contentment in connection with our agent-naturalistic account of the dignity of others, see pp. 130 *ff.*, above.

In the realm of ends, everything has either a *price* or a *dignity*. Whatever has a price can be replaced by something else as its equivalent; on the other hand, whatever is above all price, and therefore admits of no equivalent, has a dignity.

That which is related to general human inclinations and needs has a market price. That which, without presupposing any need, accords with a certain taste, i.e., with pleasure in the mere purposeless play of our faculties,[44] has an *affective price* (*Affectionspreis*). But that which constitutes the condition under which alone something can be an end in itself does not have mere relative worth, i.e., a price, but an intrinsic worth, i.e., dignity.

Now Morality is the only condition under which alone a rational being can be an end in itself; because only through it is it possible to be a legislative member in the realm of ends. Thus morality and humanity, so far as it is capable of morality, alone have dignity. (*FMM*, p. 92, AB 77.)

Human beings acquire a sense of their own dignity (and the dignity of others) in so far as they recognize themselves as beings capable of directing their behaviour according to a moral law.[45] Now if dignity only arises within the moral form of life, the reality of dignity as a genuine part of human experience would surely have to be regarded as undeniable evidence for the reality of the moral form of life. So can we offer an agent-naturalistic account of dignity when, as Kant construes it, dignity is essentially tied to the moral form of life? In order to appreciate the extent and nature of this problem, consider the difficulties which a naturalistic account of morality, such as Hume's, necessarily encounters when it tries to deal with the phenomenon of dignity.

Although Hume does not speak of dignity in so many words (there is no mention of the term in Selby-Bigge's analytical index to *A Treatise of Human Nature*), he is referring to its manifestation when he considers the question of whether "the sense of morality or duty [may] produce an action, without any other motive?"[46] Kant would agree that this is a situation in which the dignity of a person was manifested.[47] The answer

---

[44] That situation in which, according to Kant, we experience beauty. See CJ, CaJ p 58, BA 28.

[45] It is thus that "Autonomy is ... the basis of the dignity of both human nature and of every rational nature." FMM, p. 93, BA 79.

[46] David Hume, *A Treatise of Human Nature*, ed. L.A. Selby-Bigge, Clarendon Press, Oxford, 1888, p. 479.

[47] See Kant's 'Paean to Duty', CPrR, pp. 193-195, A 154-159.

Hume gives takes up the next six pages of the *Treatise* but it boils down to the following: whatever the appearance of the action may be, that is, however strongly we may feel that it was done solely out of a sense of duty, it would not be be regarded as laudable unless there was, originally at least, some *utilitarian advantage* to be gained. The effect of such an interpretation of 'dutiful' action is to discount the dignity of the act in question. It turns out that we are always—in fact—motivated by considerations which stem from natural self-interest.

On this interpretation, our dignity (considered as an unconditional value) is explained away: it is shown to be conditioned by our self-interest. On such an interpretation our feelings of duty and respect—the constituents of our dignity—must be regarded as a function of our blindness to what our real motivation is (viz. our self interest). But why are people so blind to the utilitarian roots of their 'moral' behaviour? Why do they prize, above all others, actions done out of 'higher' motives? In other words, however spurious this special feeling of human dignity may be, how is it that it presents itself as such a special feeling, special enough to ground a supernatural[47] form of life?

It is in the light of these considerations that the moralist professes to be unhappy about the reduction of moral behaviour to a species of naturally motivated behaviour. The moralist's complaint rests on a generally shared conviction that the phenomenon of dignity cannot possibly be baseless or unreal. However compelling Hume's argument may be, behaving in such a way as to put freedom and dignity aside is something that human beings find difficult even to contemplate because of their actual experience of the intrinsic value of these feelings.

This common reaction is something that the agent-naturalistic account of dignity must be able to deal with. If it is to be convincing, it must be an account which 'saves the phenomenon' and leaves us with a notion of dignity which does justice to the intrinsic value of the experience of dignity that the moralist rightly regards as crucial to human life. With this stricture in mind we can now set out the agent-naturalistic account of dignity. According to the Kantian moralist, the source of the dignity that is attributed to human beings is their recognition of themselves as

---

[47] For example, when we act out of duty we have no idea how we are able to do this, nor do we know for certain whether we have actually done it. The general difficulty we face lies in our inability to understand the basis of our capacity to act morally, namely, our freedom. To possess free will is to possess a supernatural capacity and we simply cannot understand such capacities (where by 'understand' we mean 'have the ability (more or less) to control the capacity concerned').

rational agents, beings capable of directing their behaviour according to a law. Because they recognize this capacity in themselves, they cannot pretend to themselves that passive behaviour—behaviour which is motivated by inclination— represents a fitting destiny for them. Such a pretence would necessarily be felt as intolerably shameful because it amounts to an attempt to deny to oneself what one is transparently aware of, viz. that through being able to think we have the capacity actively to determine our behaviour.

We therefore cannot pretend that we are, as agents, simply the slaves of passion, i.e. 'empirically determinable'. Indeed we cannot help but gag on such a pretence in so far as we are reflexively aware: any attempt to fool ourselves in this fashion would constitute a piece of behaviour which is ruled out by the very nature of our reflexive consciousness. The hold that our dignity has over us is not therefore something which is a consequence of our consciousness of the universal validity of the moral law, our consciousness that there is a right way to behave that is open to us. It is more basic than that. Our sense of personal worth stems from our practical awareness of our actual capacity to guide our behaviour by thinking, an activity which confers upon us the capacity to act deliberately rather than simply to react as circumstances dictate.

If we are correct in this account of the source of our personal worth, it follows that dignity, understood in this sense, confers a value on human living which is prior to the value derived from acts done solely out of the sense of duty we feel when confronted by moral laws. This priority can be understood by considering the following idea. According to Kant, I know I have done something morally wrong when I recognize that my behaviour is in conflict with a moral law, a universally valid statement about the practical consistency of a piece of behaviour. However, why do I feel any sense of compunction about doing what I have done, just as a consequence of recognizing this relationship between my behaviour and a moral law? Only, it would seem, if there was something fundamentally unpleasant about this sort of contradictory behaviour.

But from what does this unpleasantness stem? Does it simply stem from not acting rationally, from contradicting ourselves? This is what Kant thinks, but we are convinced that the roots of this unpleasantness go deeper and lie, as we have said, in our capacity to be reflexively aware. If we take 'feeling ashamed' as the common term for this unpleasantness, then we must consider whether it makes sense to regard a purely discursive awareness that what we did was wrong as its foundation (an awareness of the logical relationship between our behaviour and the moral law, viz. that the one contradicts the other). This seems to be questionable since our feelings of shame do not always arise in the context of strictly moral deliberations (those in which we recognize the validity of a moral law and see that our behaviour is at odds with this law).

Our view is that the source of our capacity to feel shame is tied to our capacity to deliberate, a capacity which necessarily involves a transparent awareness of what we are doing. Thus whenever we deliberate, we respond to the relationship between our deliberations and whatever we subsequently do, with a feeling of either shame or self-respect, feelings which reflect our awareness of how what we have done squares with our deliberations. Under the frank gaze of our reflexive awareness we are always aware of the nature of this relationship. Thus we cannot fool ourselves, and it is this basic fact about us which sets clear limits as to how we must behave if we are to be able to live with ourselves without shame or regret.

Our position, then, is that there is nothing exclusively rational about the source of that value which we refer to as our dignity. It is based on those feelings which register the relationship between what we are capable of doing if we deliberate and what we actually do. And these feelings can be present in us whether or not we consider the deliberations which guide our conduct to be universally valid. To be aware that our dignity is in jeopardy we need only be aware of a difference between what we have done and what we could, would, or should have done if we had thought about the matter more deeply. Because we have a capacity to know ourselves (to be reflexively aware) we have an inbuilt commitment to maintain our dignity, to make use of our capacity for deliberate action. This commitment is not directed at living in accordance with universally valid maxims, but instead at simply maintaining an awareness of the relationship between our actions and our deliberations. Thus agent-naturalists experience shame or self-respect according to whether they exercise their judgment when they act and not, as do moralists, according to whether what they do is in defiance of (or alternatively, in conformity with) the dictates of the moral law. Agent-naturalists are always aware that they have (or have not) done their best and are contented or ashamed as a consequence. They do not see themselves, as do moralists, as having acted rightly or wrongly, but rather as having been honest or dishonest with themselves, and this in the light of the feelings they experience as a consequence of being aware of a) the relative care with which they deliberated, and b) the accord (or lack of it) between their deliberations and their subsequent actions.

Given that this last remark is true, and given the fact that people do sometimes perform actions of which they are later ashamed, how does the agent-naturalist explain this apparent acting against one's own interests (acting in such a way as to experience the unpleasantness of shame)? For, in the nature of the case, since one is reflexively aware that one will be ashamed if one acts less deliberately, it remains a puzzle why anyone ever does so act?

It would seem that on the basis of our account the feeling of shame can only occur when, for some reason, we temporarily 'forget ourselves' so to speak. Typically this happens when we become so completely absorbed in what we are doing that we cease, or almost cease, to be reflexively aware of the fact that we are just blindly following our inclinations.[49] For without reflexive awareness we cannot deliberate and thus cannot make a judgment as to where our true interest lies. Afterwards, when we again become conscious (or simply *more* conscious) of the shortsightedness of our behaviour, we feel ashamed to have thus 'forgotten ourselves', to have forgotten our capacity to think before we act. With this onset of reflexive consciousness we suddenly become aware of the fact that we cannot countenance such passive (uncontrolled) behaviour in ourselves and immediately regret the fact that we somehow lost that sense of perspective and control which reflexive consciousness makes possible.

Our sense of shame thus implies that we have a responsibility for what we have failed to do. It marks us out as creatures who labour under a kind of ontological imperative telling us what to do in terms of what we are or could be. This imperative would run something like this: 'Ceaselessly maintain yourself in a reflexive state of consciousness since only in such a state of being can you judge whether a given line of action is in your own true interest'. However the fact that we do occasionally act in such a way as subsequently to feel ashamed indicates to us that, as finite agents, we can comply with this ontological imperative only more or less successfully. To avoid feeling ashamed (or more accurately, to reduce the frequency of such lapses) we must, therefore, endeavour to train ourselves using psychological techniques[50] so that we naturally revert to a reflexive state of consciousness whenever the situation confronting us

---

[49] This often happens, for example, in sporting contests when people behave in ways which they later regret.

[50] See pp. 77 ff. above, where Spinoza's techniques for accomplishing this psychological training are mentioned.

is such that (on the basis of past experience) we know that the consequences of such actions will matter to us.

It is worth noting that engaging in such endeavours—more or less consistently—is essentially what being 'grown-up' amounts to, for as Aristotle rightly remarks:

> The feeling [of shame] is not becoming to every age, but only to youth. For we think young people should be prone to the feeling of shame because they live by feeling and therefore commit many errors, but are restrained by shame; and we praise young people who are prone to this feeling, but an older person no one would praise for being prone to the sense of disgrace, since we think he should not do anything that need cause this sense.[50]

In our terms, the older person should not be prone to the sense of disgrace because that person should have developed the disposition to reflect before acting.

Dignity has, therefore, an agent-naturalistic explanation. The thing that we maintain when we maintain our dignity is our capacity to reflect on our actions, a capacity with which we are naturally endowed in so far as we have the capacity to be reflexively aware. In such a state we can never act blindly (passively) nor can we pretend to ourselves that we can. Our sense of being a person, our sense of self-respect, our sense of dignity, are all explained by this fact that we cannot, as reflexive beings, pretend to be what we (transparently) are not.

Thus, on the agent-naturalistic account, the special quality of human dignity—the dignity that attaches to a being who is capable of being reflexively aware—is intrinsic to our nature as knowing beings, beings with a capacity to deliberate and act. Thus such an explanation 'saves the phenomenon' in that dignity for the agent-naturalist retains the significant characteristics of dignity as the moralist understands this notion. The agent-naturalist's notion has, at its core, the characterization of dignity as an intrinsic value: it has no market price to use Kant's phrase. Nothing can compensate a person for feeling ashamed (i.e. for the loss of his or her dignity). However, on the agent-naturalist's account, this idea is already a natural function of our unavoidable knowledge of the relative inadequacy of our deliberations (when we feel

---

[50] See Aristotle, 'Nichomechean Ethics', translated by Sir David Ross, in *The Basic Works of Aristotle*, ed. Richard McKeon, Random House, New York, 1941, p. 1001, 1128b 15-21.

ashamed of ourselves). So there is no need to suppose that the intrinsic value of dignity must rest upon a uniquely moral function—our capacity to act rationally in the strict sense, to act only in accordance with maxims which possess universal validity according to the criterion laid down by the Categorical Imperative. Indeed, we maintain that it makes more sense to think that moral dignity is itself superimposed upon natural dignity and derives its intrinsic value (its priceless significance to us as human beings) from this natural source. In any case, the agent-naturalistic conception of dignity provides an account of human dignity which can stand independently of the moral conception, and in the course of subsequent arguments, we hope to show that it constitutes a more satisfying account of dignity than that provided by Kant.

The Dignity of Others

In order to substantiate this let us now turn to the question of the dignity of others. The agent-naturalistic account of dignity is directed towards the problem of explaining how it is that, as (finite) conscious agents, we have a sense of personal worth. We have argued that this sense of personal worth is a function of our capacity to act more or less deliberately. Because we are aware of this capacity to exercise a degree of control over our activities, we must acknowledge that we have a natural responsibility for what we do which our sense of shame supervises vigilantly.

But what about the dignity of others? According to Kant, we have a moral duty to treat other people "never merely as means but in every case also as an end in [themselves]."[51] Kant bases this view on the inviolable character of the moral law (based on its universality and thus on the practical contradiction involved in excepting ourselves from it in so far as we are, as rational creatures, necessarily obliged to count ourselves as falling under its edict) and, by extension, on the inviolable status of any creature capable of directing itself in accordance with it.[52] This respect for the dignity of others is perhaps the most important aspect of morality. For most of us, moral behaviour is simply identified with that kind of behaviour which takes due concern for other people's lives and that therefore, when we think about what we should do, we should never presume other people's lives to be unimportant. And if we now ask whether other people's lives matter in an absolute sense we touch the

[51] FMM, p. 91, BA 74.
[52] ibid, p. 93, BA 78-79.

moral nerve of Kant's position. For Kant the lives of all rational agents have an *inviolable* status. Under no circumstances is it permissible to ignore the inherent dignity which their rational agency confers upon them.

What then can the agent-naturalist offer as an alternative account of this moral sanction which regulates our dealings with each other in such a central fashion?

A naturalistic explanation of other-regarding behaviour normally tends toward some version of Hume's theory that such behaviour stems from our natural sympathy with other human beings:

. . . moral distinctions arise, in a great measure, from the tendency of qualities and characters to the interests of society, and that 'tis our concern for that interest, which makes us approve or disapprove of them. Now we have no such extensive concern for society but from sympathy; and consequently 'tis that principle, which takes us so far out of ourselves, as to give us the same pleasure or uneasiness in the characters of others, as if they had a tendency to our own advantage or loss.[53]

The whole scheme...of law and justice is advantageous to the society; and 'twas with a view to this advantage, that men, by their voluntary conventions, establish'd it. After it was once established by these conventions, it is *naturally* attended with a strong sentiment of morals; which can proceed from nothing but our sympathy with the interests of society. We need no other explication of that esteem, which attends such of the natural virtues, as have a tendency to the public good.[54]

For Hume, other people's lives matter because our own feelings are naturally in tune with theirs and since, by definition, our feelings matter to us, then by extension the fate of every other person matters to us:

As in strings equally wound up, the motion of one communicates itself to the rest; so all the affections readily pass from one person to another, and beget correspondent movements in every human creature.[55]

Inevitably Hume's theory boils down to the view that other-regarding behaviour is motivated by self-regarding behaviour. It is my feeling of

---

[53] David Hume, *A Treatise of Human Nature*, ed. L. A. Selby-Bigge, Clarendon Press, Oxford, 1888, p.579.
[54] ibid., pp. 579-580.
[55] ibid., p. 576.

uneasiness (communicated sympathetically through my imagination of the uneasiness of others) that motivates my 'moral' behaviour towards other people.

On such a view, no new kind of value is created by respecting the rights of others, by treating them with dignity. The motive of such behaviour is inevitably *my* happiness, the alleviation of *my* sympathetic uneasiness of mind. And it would seem that the moralist has a right to complain (yet again) that this sort of naturalistic explanation does not capture our intuitive sense of the *intrinsic* value that attaches to each person's life, a value which we bring into being when we treat other people with dignity. It is not surprising, then, that the moralist should insist that our recognition of another person's intrinsic value (their dignity) is not a function of fellow-feeling or sympathy, but a function of our conception of them as autonomous rational agents.

However, because the moralist insists that the dignity of other people lies in their capacity for autonomous behaviour, it would seem that our moral duty towards other people is essentially a negative one. We must not use them as a means only (without any reference to their status as ends in themselves, a status dependent upon their autonomy): we must not interfere with their capacity to realize their autonomy in moral (or immoral) actions. The moralist's respect for other individuals rests on a conception of them as free individuals, as self-sufficient captains of their souls, autonomous sources of moral value.

Now in opposition to this view we would argue that, in reality, finite agents do not find themselves to be self-sufficient. Instead, as a general rule, we find that our capacity for autonomous behaviour is by no means an absolute capacity. When we think about our capacity to control our behaviour we can never be in doubt about our own finitude: we are certainly *more or less* in control of what we do but that is all. Thus our respect for the dignity of other agents (given the assumption that they are like us) cannot rest on any straightforward recognition of such a self-sufficient capacity in others.[56] One possibility (according to the agent-naturalist) is that the special value the finite agent attributes to other agents may be based on the fact that, when finite agents *interact* harmoniously, they are together able to be more active (to experience an increased sense of their control over what they are doing). They thereby experience together the unique kind of happiness which graces such

---

[56] If we think we see this capacity in others we lose our kinship with them, which rests on our finiteness and thus our mutual acceptance that each agent should act in reciprocal harmony with every other.

mutual endeavours. Such happiness would have a preeminent value since it is superior (in some obvious way) to the kind of happiness that agents can experience as a result of their independent endeavours. Perhaps it is this fact about human agents—the need they have for each other if they are to experience this special kind of happiness—that explains the intrinsic value which the agent-naturalist attributes to all human agents. It is worth noting that the agent-naturalist attributes value to other agents on the basis of something through which agents *lose* their distinct individuality—their capacity to interact harmoniously.

The moralist, by contrast, attributes dignity to others in virtue of that characteristic which allows the human individual to be uniquely self-sufficient—autonomy. And yet these opposing views do have a common feature. In both, the attribution of intrinsic value to the agent rests on the agent's possession of an innate capacity (a capacity that essentially defines the being of that agent). As we have mentioned before and will have reason to note again, intrinsic values—*moral* values—have ontological roots: they involve a recognition of the overriding importance of the ontological status of the agent concerned as the determining factor in how it should behave and be treated and this is why it is in virtue of this status that the moralist, and the agent-naturalist, attribute intrinsic value to human agents.

It is clear that these two views of agency find their deepest opposition where they consider the individual agent in its relation to other agents. The moralist's view is fundamentally solipsistic. Like Henley's famous captain[57], moral agents stand alone against nature and stand essentially unconnected with the other autonomous captains. All of them fight the good fight as individuals. Their respect for each other is an extension of their self-respect. For it is the assumption that the others are autonomous, as they themselves are, that grounds the conception they have of the dignity of other agents. The agent-naturalist's view is that the finite agent discovers its status as an agent (and thus the proper conception of its dignity) only in so far as it recognizes its finitude and thus its essential need to cooperate with others, a need essential to the fulfilment of its destiny as an integral part of nature. In Spinoza's view, our dignity as agents is a function of our coming to understand our place

---

[57] *The Oxford Book Of Victorian Verse*, chosen by Arthur Quiller-Couch, Oxford, Clarendon Press, 1919, p. 722:
  "It matters not how strait the gate,
  How charged with punishments the scroll
  I am the master of my fate:
  I am the captain of my soul."

in nature and involves an acceptance of our status or, as he puts it, an acquiescence in what we are.[58]

In keeping with these views, the special satisfaction that the moralist gains from behaving dutifully (solely out of respect for the moral law) is *self*-contentment, a satisfaction necessarily confined to ourselves in that it is constituted by our "consciousness of mastery over inclinations and thus of independence from them and from the discontentment which always accompanies them."[59] Now by contrast, when the finite agent acts in accordance with the requirements of its dignity (that one must act in reciprocal cooperation with others in order to be true to one's nature) and therefore strives to interact harmoniously with its complement, it experiences (in a degree relative to the success of this endeavour) a shared satisfaction distinctive of successful interaction. Perhaps the best word for this experience is 'joy', but whatever word one might use to describe it, this joint sense of satisfaction that arises from cooperative endeavour presents an intriguing contrast with the self-contentment of the moralist. Thus depending on one's conception of where the dignity of a human agent lies, one can expect quite different sorts of satisfactions if one lives with dignity.

On this agent-naturalistic view, other agents *complement* our capacity to endeavour and thereby increase the control we together have over our joint endeavours. In so doing, they contribute to the *mutual* satisfaction (joy) we take in this increased level of activity. However is this agent-naturalistic view of the status (dignity) of other agents an adequate substitute for the moralist's view of other people, the view that accords them a dignity? In some respects it is. The value that the agent-naturalist sets on other people has no marketprice in the sense that there is no substitute for another person if we are to mitigate our finitude by joining with our complement and thereby become a 'larger individual', with greater powers (and greater satisfactions). However, in other respects it is not. There is, after all, one obvious substitute for another person and that is some other person. The agent-naturalist recognizes that we need other people to flourish, but clearly some individuals will complement us better than others and this raises a sticky point.

Attempts to interact harmoniously with some people do not provide mutual satisfaction. One of the parties (the party of the first part) may be enjoying the (so far as they are concerned) shared endeavour, but the other may not find that their capacity to endeavour is being increased through

---

[58] See *Ethics*, p. 178, III Definitions of Emotions XXV.
[59] *CPrR*, p. 222, A213.

this joint effort. They may find no joy in it and therefore see no reason why they should not cease to act as a complement to the other agent. Would such an action amount to a denial of the intrinsic value of the party of the first part—a denial of their dignity? Do we have a duty to help others whatever the cost to ourselves? And if we do, is it a moral duty as Kant understands this notion?

At first glance, it might be thought that Kant thinks that it is a moral duty on the grounds that (were we to be the party of the first part) we would certainly wish others to help us whether or not this action on their part proved to be enjoyable for them. However, in the examples he cites, Kant is clearly thinking of helping in the sense of lending temporary aid: suppose you find yourself hungry and in need of food, or trapped in a car accident and in need of rescue. There is no doubt that, under these circumstances, Kant thinks that you have a moral duty to help since it would be self-contradictory (in the sense that it would be unrealistic) to pretend that you yourself would not will that others should help you were you to be in their place.[60] And the agent-naturalist can agree with this description of these facts about our finitude: we are not self-sufficient. We will need help from time to time. We have therefore a duty—based on our recognition of our finitude as human beings—to recognize the finitude of others and act accordingly in the hope that others will feel the same way when they see that we are in trouble.

But what about the really difficult situation in which the party of the first part is just as described originally, viz. someone who clearly enjoys 'mutually' endeavouring with you but with whom you do not share this feeling. Do you have a moral duty to continue 'sharing' in this endeavour, to continue being *nice* to people who fail (as a matter of fact) to be suitable complements to your particular capacity to endeavour? On Kant's view we clearly have such a duty. We could not will (without insincerity) that other people should not put some effort into being nice to us when interaction does not come easily. However it may appear that agent-naturalism does not require us to expend any more concern on people as soon as we find we are not being complemented by them.[61] It seems that we have a natural duty to treat everyone else with the respect due to their status as agents with whom we share, on account of our mutual finitude, the potential to engage in some kind of jointly satisfactory endeavour. However we have no duty, it seems, to 'go the

---

[60] See FMM, p. 82, BA 56-57.
[61] This would seem to be the basis of Spinoza's rather disdainful view of pity. See Ethics, p. 221, IV Proposition L.

second mile'. Such a judgment is, however, premature—a function of an incomplete appreciation of what it means to be a finite agent—and, indeed, it is to combat this very tendency to judge prematurely that the moralist approach finds its soundest rationale. As finite, a human agent can never know *with certainty* that it cannot and will not, in the long term (and even sometimes in the short term), interact harmoniously with another agent. It is a presumption to take it upon oneself to write off another person as an unsuitable complement.

The natural dignity which we all possess as finite agents is a function of our capacity to raise each other's endeavours to a new pitch of activity. Because we are finite, we must acknowledge that others have a value as potential complements to a degree that we can never ascertain with certainty. We therefore must, to the limits of our ability, treat everyone as worthy of our concern, or at least, avoid any deliberate move to disregard others just for our own immediate comfort. For we can see that even our own dignity is a function of our ability to interact as complements to others. Thus we do not gain our conception of dignity through an examination of our own status as individuals and somehow allow this conception of our dignity to spread to others by analogy. Instead we begin with the idea that the worth of all agents, ourselves included, derives from the necessity that they should realize their essential nature through interaction with others. To discount the value of others is to risk harm to all, including oneself, by challenging the basic presumption upon which the natural dignity of every agent rests, namely, that we all need one another if we are to realize our true natures.

Spontaneity and Freedom

Our discussion of morality as a form of life has, among other things, indicated that this form of life does not warrant our treating it with the sanctity which is usually accorded to it. We have argued that the unique value of morality can be 'explained away' in terms of an agent-naturalistic conception of human endeavour which serves as an adequate and a preferable[63] alternative for this form of life.

An obvious presumption of the enterprise of explaining away morality is that morality in itself is a bad thing. It is presumed that it somehow distorts our nature, encouraging us to behave in ways which can only frustrate us. Thus, for example, although there is an easily understood

---

[63] It is preferable, for example, because the conception of human agency that it is based upon fits the facts more adequately than its rival.

agent-naturalistic interpretation of the rubric 'ought implies can',[63] there is no intelligible reading for the moral interpretation of this notion. For there to be an 'intelligible' basis for our being able to do as we ought, we must be accounted free. Yet the exercise of our freedom, or rather our understanding of *how* we can exercise it (how respect for the moral law can become an incentive for us), remains opaque. As Kant himself says:

> For how a law in itself can be the direct determining ground of the will (which is the essence of morality) is an insoluble problem for the human reason. It is identical with the problem of how a free will is possible. (*CPrR*, p. 180, A 128)

We can only understand this phenomenon of freedom as an implication of the moral form of life: we cannot grasp it as a working tool with which to organize our lives.

Human freedom, then, is a mystery. But is it correct to say therefore that human beings are basically mysterious creatures? Agent-naturalism assumes the negative, but this assumption needs to be justified. After all, from the fact that we cannot understand the mystery of freedom it does not follow that there is not, in fact, a mystery here. Indeed the very fact that we cannot understand this 'freedom' could well be taken to indicate that there is something at the heart of our being which is essentially beyond our ken. After all, how did this idea gain its currency in the first place if there is not some fire behind all the smoke?

To rephrase the question, if, as the agent-naturalist is so eager to point out, morality as a form of life is at bottom unintelligible, how is it that we ever adopted it as a form of life in the first place? If the language game which expresses its essence is unintelligible, how did we learn to play it? Even if we are right in explaining away morality as a phenomenon superimposed upon a natural and unmysterious conception of human agency, the question of why this superimposition ever took place needs an answer. Why did morality emerge to cloud our natural conception of our being (as finite agents with a limited capacity to control our behaviour)?

This line of thought presents us with an obvious problem: throughout the discussion we have been assuming that we can discern—in a straightforward manner—the essentials of human nature. We have assumed that it is obvious what the natural capacities of a human being are and therefore

---

[63] See Chapter Four. Judgmental feelings tell us what we 'ought' to do and as feelings enable us to act. There is no practical (or logical) problem involved in moving from this sort of 'ought' to the action it counsels.

is obvious what the natural capacities of a human being are and therefore in what way this nature has been distorted by an incorrect conception of it. Our criterion for making such judgments on the nature of our agency has been this. Where we can (to some extent) control our behaviour through some technique, we have assumed that this kind of behaviour is natural to us. It is a capacity we actually possess. This is why 'freedom' is regarded as a supernatural capacity: we do not possess a technique for exercising it. But now we must ask: does it follow that because we cannot understand our capacity to act freely (because we do not know how to control it 'technically') we lack such a capacity? In other words, is it safe to assume that the criterion we are using actually possesses the power we have assumed it to possess, namely, the power to dictate that nature must be synonymous with its intelligible description?

The problem can be illustrated with respect to a marginal phenomenon like pre-cognition. When people dream and a day later find that some experience conforms to their dream, they may think they have a natural ability to tell the future. However, do we allow that they actually possess this capacity, if, as it happens, they possess no technique for controlling their ability to predict the future? It seems that if they cannot bring about—more or less at will— this experience of having correct predictive dreams, we are forced to disregard their claim that they possess such a capacity, effectively dismissing the supposition that such a capacity could be a part of nature. Our attitude is, in a nutshell: 'There are no mysteries in nature, only (so far) unexplained phenomena.'

The virtue of this approach seems to be widely recognized. Thus while pre-cognition is still a mystery, witchcraft, for example, no longer is. 'Witches' have pretty well 'disappeared' from nature. They have been explained away.

The character of such a view is revealed in the single quotation marks which it contains: 'witches' have 'disappeared' only in the sense that it is now widely acknowledged that individuals with witch-like powers never were a part of nature. This is not, of course, to say that, when witches were still a genuine mystery, they were then a part of nature. Certainly people used to think there were witches because they thought they knew how to recognize a witch. However, as time went on, it was discovered that the criteria for recognizing a witch could not be relied upon to distinguish witches from ordinary folk. The form of life fell into disrepute and 'witches' 'disappeared'.

Could we tell an analogous story about morality? Is it possible that one day the following tale could be told about the 'old days': 'People used to think that human beings possessed a free will which they exercised when they acted morally. They believed that they could tell moral behaviour from behaviour that had the appearance of moral behaviour but was in fact governed by heteronomous causes (also known as "ulterior motives") rather than free decisions. However it was gradually realized that they could not tell the difference and so the distinction fell into disrepute. It finally became clear that all human actions have motives and that it was silly to imagine that some do not. Free will (the causal foundation of morality) never was a capacity which agents actually possessed.'

To what extent does the imagined analogy seem acceptable? One key disanalogy lies in the question of technique. There were techniques in the practice of witchcraft (e.g. making effigies of an enemy and then destroying these figures with the intention of destroying the enemy through the 'sympathetic' connection that had been established *via* the effigy), but they did not work in the sense that they failed to operate in that reliable (repeatable at will) fashion that establishes a practice as effective and therefore signals its status as a real phenomenon. However, in the Kantian form of moral theory, there is no such thing as a technique for exercising our freedom, our capacity to create moral value. There has never been a period in history when people thought they knew *how* to go about creating the kind of moral value Kant champions. Does anyone know how it is possible to act *solely* out of respect for the moral law? Or do we know how to choose to do what is right *simply because* it is right? It is clear that no one knows how to be good, although they may understand very well what it is to be good.[65]

But if no technique for being good is even offered, how is it that human beings ever acquired so much as the notion of moral value, let alone the confidence that they could exercise the capacity to create this value, at will? Since there are, it seems, no techniques available through which a person could learn how to choose the good freely, understanding how we could have learned the meaning of terms like 'free' and 'moral'

---

[65] It might be objected here that we are overlooking the fact that being able to do something does not imply that we know how to do it. I may be able to make you laugh though I do not know how I am able to do it in the sense that I possess no reliable technique for eliciting laughter from you. But by the same token, I do not feel that I am responsible—i.e. deserving of blame—if this spontaneous capacity of mine does not work. And this is the difficulty with spontaneous exercises of free will. Though they are spontaneous, I am held morally responsible for them, but how can I be if I am not able deliberately to control them through some technique which I know how to activate. We thank Roy Perrett for raising this point.

presents us with a mystery and anything mysterious cries out for a natural explanation. Spinoza claims to provide such an explanation. Let us examine it to see whether it will suffice:

> For instance, men are mistaken in thinking themselves free; their opinion is made up of consciousness of their own actions, and ignorance of the causes by which they are conditioned. Their idea of freedom, therefore, is simply their ignorance of any cause for their actions. As for their saying that human actions depend on the will, this is a mere phrase without any idea to correspond thereto. What the will is, and how it moves the body, they none of them know; those who boast of such knowledge, and feign dwellings and habitations for the soul, are wont to provoke either laughter or disgust. (*Ethics*, p.108-109, II Proposition XXXV Note.)

It is our consciousness of our own actions and our ignorance of their causes that leaves room for the idea of freedom to gain a foothold. Through these notions I know how to apply the concept of freedom to my conduct. Using them I can readily distinguish between those actions which—by default of other causes—are my doing and those to which I can actually attribute specific causes. On the agent-naturalistic conception of human agency, freedom in this sense is a term that is used negatively. I describe my actions, for instance, as free, in the sense of being undetermined, when my consciousness of acting is not accompanied by a consciousness of my actions flowing from various causes.

Strictly speaking, then, I should use the word 'free' to describe those activities which I engage in spontaneously—as it seems to me. Since I have no explanation for them (being ignorant of their causes) I pigeonhole them under the notion of 'free acts'.[66] However if I take this attitude towards free acts it would seem to follow that I should deprive them of any value as human actions since I would not, by definition, be aware of how I came to act in this way on this occasion. As *un*-considered acts (not ill- or well-considered) their value could only lie in their unforeseen consequences. They could not have any value derived from the frame of mind of the agent who effected them, since this frame of mind (e.g. respect for the moral law) is only 'effective' if I will in accordance with this feeling, and I do not know how I determine myself

---

[66] Thus on the agent-naturalistic interpretation, 'free' acts (in the sense of free = undetermined) are simply a subset of the class of caused events, viz. those caused events of which I am ignorant of their causes.

to do this. Sometimes I just am able to do it, and sometimes not. But why should moral value be created by such spontaneous acts?

Thus, in the wake of the agent-naturalistic explanation of how it is that we know when to apply the term 'free' to a given action, the 'mystery' about the crucial role of freedom in the moral form of life shifts to the question of why it is that spontaneous action should have any value at all. Why should spontaneity be the capacity which allows human agents to create moral value? It is not at all evident why our consciousness of not knowing how we were able to act solely out of respect for the moral law should be a mark of value. The moralist certainly does not want to take this view. What is it then about free actions which marks them out as value-creating?

Now there is a situation in which we attach value to spontaneous activities, a value which stems from the nature of the act rather than its consequences, and to that extent, it fits in with the paradigm of free acts as having an intrinsic value: thus if I freely (=spontaneously) give, or refuse to give, help to someone in need, the nature of the aid (its value to the person) is one thing, but the value which attaches to the spontaneity of my act is quite another. Its value lies in the evidence it provides as to the natural tendency towards generosity, or meanness, which I thereby display. It is clear that it is not a Kantian moral value, since the act is not incited by any conscious consideration of the principle involved. If it were incited by a consideration of the rightness of so acting, it would lose the spontaneity which creates the natural value we attach to the act. (It would instead have a moral value.) For it is a person's natural tendency towards kindness which we value in a spontaneous act of generosity, not their moral rectitude. However, despite this difference, the natural value we attach to spontaneous acts is related to that potential for moral behaviour which Kant considered a necessary presuppostion of the possibility of the creation of moral value, viz. that the will's being determined to act in accordance with the moral law must be an act of absolute spontaneity. As Kant maintains,

...freedom of the will is of a wholly unique nature in that an incentive can determine the will to an action *only so far as the individual has incorporated it into his maxim* (has made it the general rule in accordance with which he will conduct himself); only thus can an incentive, whatever it may be, co-exist with the absolute spontaneity of the will (i.e., freedom). (RWL, p. 19, A 10 B 12.)

This relation between the natural value we attach to a free (=spontaneous)

act and moral value is worth considering further.[66] It is important because the value of spontaneous activity is a natural value which is distinct from the utilitarian values which may or may not stem from its consequences (values stemming from the wisdom of the act). Spontaneous kindness sometimes leads to unpleasant consequences, but despite this fact it is still something we value in human beings, apparently for its own sake. (Though, as Hume would, doubtless, insist,[67] we would not regard it as having any 'intrinsic' value if it did not generally have utility value.) Bearing in mind this qualification, the phenomenon of spontaneous kindness (and our regard for the 'beauty of the act' apart from the detail of its consequences) could be regarded as the natural value underpinning moral values. Specifically, it could be seen as underpinning those values which are said to stem from acts of free will and which are valued regardless of what consequences might flow from them. If this argument is allowed as having *some* plausibility it could then be used to show that the natural value attaching to spontaneity may be regarded as the phenomenological basis for the distinctive moral value which, morality declares, stems from the fact that all moral activity is, at bottom, freely undertaken. In other words, the value that moralists place on our freedom of choice may, in fact, be quite intelligible through being grounded in the value we naturally attach to spontaneous actions.[68]

Now it is true that the value of moral activities is not totally characterized by this spontaneous element in the sense that the spontaneity which they have is not valued simply for its unconsidered character. The moral value of a free moral choice stems from the fact that, when we freely undertake to perform moral activities, we know why we are choosing to behave in that particular way. We have moral *reasons*, but nevertheless, the spontaneity of the decision—our willingness in the moment of decision to be guided by these reasons—can never itself be

---

[66] This relates to the distinction in Kant, highlighted by Beck (in *A Commentary on Kant's Critique of Practical Reason*, University of Chicago Press, Chicago, 1960, p. 176 ff.) between *Willkur* and *Wille*. *Willkur* is will as choice. It responds to the moral law which is given to it by *Wille*, this being the purely rational aspect of the will, or will as pure practical reason. *Wille* is the capacity to be *moral*: it provides the moral imperative. *Willkur* is the capacity to make a free response to this imperative, to actually *be* moral.

[67] David Hume, *A Treatise of Human Nature*, ed. L. A. Selby-Bigge, Clarendon Press, Oxford, 1888, p. 603-604.

[68] Note that it is not just utilitarian acts of spontaneity that we value. We often value spontaneity in itself, as opposed to predictability and dullness. It is spontaneity which we appreciate when we value inventiveness, imaginativeness, sparkle, etc

attributed to these reasons. The moral law can be presented to us as a valid objective principle, but we ourselves must make this principle our own—make it a subjective[69] principle—so that we can act on it. It is up to us to relate the objective (and thus personally neutral) principle to ourselves, to show that it is something that matters to us. Only then can the moral law become the reason that we act as we do.

Now, of necessity, we cannot say how it is that we choose to be good (or choose not to) any more than we could say why we were, on a given occasion, spontaneously kind (or uncaring). The actual exercise of our freedom remains a mystery to us. Therefore the wonderful (or disturbing) thing about the exercise of our freedom is *that* we actually make these choices: we either incorporate the moral law into our subjective maxim or we do not. The moral value of this exercise of our capacity to choose is actually created by a preferring, a valuing (of the moral law), and this, in its very nature (within the moral form of life), must be spontaneous from the point of view of our understanding of how it came about. Otherwise there would be a natural explanation for our choice and then our choosing the way we do would have no moral value.

Now let us return for a moment to the fact that we naturally accord value to spontaneous activities. Part of the natural beauty of a spontaneous act of, for example, generosity lies (as we mentioned above) in its unconsidered nature. Its very spontaneity ensures that the act was, as a matter of fact, free from any thought of personal gain. This consideration provides the firm link we are seeking between the natural beauty of such an unconsidered act, and the moral value which we accord to an act done solely out of respect for the moral law. For a corollary of acting out of respect alone is that the act be done with no thought of personal gain.

In the first case, the lack of any thought related to personal gain is guaranteed by the evident spontaneity of the action. The fact that it is regarded as an unconsidered act guarantees its 'purity' in this regard. In the second case, however, there is a sense in which the thought of personal gain is always present as the converse of the thought which makes the act a moral act, viz. the thought that we are under an obligation to act *solely* out of respect for the moral law. No wonder then that it is difficult for people to tell whether, on a given occasion, they have succeeded in acting morally. A 'subreptive' influence—the thought of personal gain—is always a consideration which is analytically present

---

[69] For this distinction in Kant see FMM, p. 62 n. BA 16 n.; cf. RWL, p. 19, A 10 B 12, quoted immediately above.

when we try to act morally and it necessarily spoils the purity of the act: how, after all, can I say with confidence that the thought of personal gain—though present—had no part to play in my behaviour?[71]

A curious reversal has now taken place. We at first supposed that the value we accorded to (unconsidered) spontaneous behaviour was the natural ground upon which the moralist built the contention that an action must be freely taken to have any moral value. However, it now seems that the value we naturally accord to such spontaneous acts has a moral flavour. It is their freedom from any thought of personal gain which accounts, in part, for their value. As a matter of fact they have no moral value because they are not the result of deliberate choices. And yet, paradoxically, their spontaneous (unconsidered) character wins our approbation because they succeed by default in manifesting a 'frame of mind' which is, in part, the frame of mind required by the moral form of life. But, of course, such acts are done without any thought of personal gain because they are done without any thought, period. Their natural value—as opposed to the 'moral' value they have by default—stems from our delight in the fact that the person involved is naturally 'good': the person shows a spontaneous tendency to interact harmoniously with other people.

Moreover, it must be appreciated that such acts have no moral value in terms of the kind of morality espoused by the agent-naturalist. The agent-naturalist is certainly pleased with such evidence of natural goodness but, like the Kantian moralist, there is an unwillingness to say that spontaneous acts of this sort have any moral value. Agent-naturalism discerns moral value where the agent's actions are the results of a considered judgment: the more consideration given, the more moral value it will assign to the agent's endeavours. There is, of course, always some degree of spontaneity in an agent's taking a particular line, simply because, as finite, the agent must in the end make a judgment on the basis of information which cannot by itself determine which direction the agent will take. Judgments must be made responsibly to have any moral value and our assumption of the responsibility for them involves the exercise of our agency in a spontaneous act of the understanding, viz. a judgment through which we *create* a rule to govern our present conduct. In other words, there is always an element of spontaneity (= creativity) in

---

[71] cf. *FMM*, p. 67, BA 27: "Out of love for humanity I am willing to admit that most of our actions are in accordance with duty; but, if we look closer at our thoughts and aspirations, we everywhere come upon the dear self, which is always salient, and it is this instead of the stern command of duty (which would often require self-denial) which supports our plans."

a normal person's judgments. It is in virtue of this that people feel that they must take responsibility for the value judgment they have made. The assumption of responsibility for the results of their considerations is evidence for the fact that they are agents who are more or less in control of their behaviour and who are thus willing to stand by their judgments and live according to the rules that such judgments put in place as maxims according to which we are to act under the present circumstances. Thus for the agent-naturalist, the intrinsic value of spontaneity—thought of as the capacity to make a judgment—is the declaration that we make when we exercise this capacity, a declaration that we are willing to take responsibility for the exercise of this spontaneity. We are able, as agents, to *make* those judgments about what we should do through the deliberate exercise of our finite capacity to make a judgment. Evidence of a person's capacity to make up his or her mind is evidence that the person concerned is normal, in the natural possession of those powers to exert control over behaviour that we call sanity.

For the agent-naturalist, evidence of this kind of spontaneity is simply evidence that the agent is more or less active, more or less in control of its life. Where there is an evident lack of spontaneity, where people seem to have difficulty making judgments and are uneasy about accepting responsibility for their activities, there the agent-naturalist sees signs of abnormality (dis-ease)—signs that the people in question are being more or less passive in regard to the control of their lives.

However, in contradistinction to all this, moralists treat this spontaneity that initiates action as the locus of a controlled choice, not a judgment. They see it as a moment in which an instantaneous act of selecting between naturally incommensurable options occurs. If this choice is in line with the moral law, the value created is called 'goodness' and the moralist delights in the fact that the agent *decided* to be good and did not—simply as a matter of fact—turn out to be good.

What then separates the Kantian and the agent-naturalist positions? The evidence of human behaviour, whether we gather it introspectively or through the observation of other people, seems neutral. The same situation which wins the agent-naturalist's approval, one in which there is evidence of a relatively active participation of the agent in controlling its life, will be the very situation in which the moralist will approve the fact that the agent freely made a decision to be good. A decision as to which characterization accurately depicts our nature as human beings will depend upon whether one believes that there is, ultimately, a free act of will through which we decide what is to matter to us or, alternatively, whether one thinks that these 'free' choices can be adequately understood as the 'spontaneous', i.e. natural, outcome of deliberation. In the end it seems to be a matter of the moralist insisting that there is more to choice than just the judgmental process of arriving at our preferences, more to it than simply considering the situation and judging where, so far as we can see, our true interest lies.

Why then does the moralist think that there is 'more to it'? For example, Kant makes a distinction between being good and being kind and at the same time insists that we can never, in fact, make such a distinction with certainty[72] (whether in our own case or in that of another agent). (Agent-naturalism does not have this problem. People are judged to be kind when they are moved by their feelings. They are judged to be good when they are moved by their judgmental feelings, and we have no difficulty distinguishing between these two cases.) Yet for Kant it is vital to distinguish, in theory at least, between being motivated by feelings (such as kindness) and acting out of respect for the moral law.[73] But why maintain a distinction in theory when there is no practical means of employing it? What are we to do when a theory declares that there is a humanly[74] undetectable difference between two modes of behaviour and insists that it is a difference which makes all the difference?

In the last chapter we will make a further attempt to explain the attractions of the moral life which are tied so intimately with the question of freedom.

---

[72] See pp. 54 *ff.*, above, on the matter of subreption.

[73] The clarification of this distinction is the chief purpose of the Analytic in the CPrR.

[74] Note that Kant endeavours to resolve this by postulating immortality and God as Judge (detector of the empirically undetectable), so that in theory it becomes possible to distinguish them. It is clear, however, that this fails to touch on any possibility "in this life" (CPrR, p. 219, A 207) as well as doing a severe injustice to the Christian tradition from which it is drawn.

CHAPTER EIGHT

THE UNIQUE VIABILITY OF THE MORAL FORM OF LIFE

Our general thesis throughout has been that morality as a form of life is superimposed upon (and therefore may be explained away by) an agent-naturalistic conception of human behaviour. However, this thesis raises the question of why this superimposition takes place at all and why this form of life (even though superimposed) is so resistant to any efforts to explain it away. It seems as if the internal coherence of this form of life renders it capable of an independent existence, permitting it to float, as it were, above the agent-naturalistic interpretation which seeks to bring it down to earth. Can we then offer any explanation of the unique viability of morality, its singular capacity to survive all efforts to explain it away? We think that the following considerations may hold the key to this problem.

Let us begin by exploring the idea of the ontological imperative[1] viz. *Be what you are.* As it stands, the force of this imperative is irresistible. Its tautological content makes it uninteresting from a practical point of view, since it leaves no room for any deliberation concerning what I ought to do to fulfill it. The imperative constitutes an injunction which is fulfilled whatever the agent does. However, the ontological imperative can be expanded in two ways, both of which can intelligibly present themselves as practical injunctions. The first is: 'Be what you *essentially* are' and the second: 'Be what you *in fact* are.' The first constitutes the prototype of a moral imperative, the second is the prototypical statement of the imperative which informs the agent-naturalistic conception of morality.

The moral reading of the ontological imperative sets in train a dialectic of the following form. In the first place the assumption that there is an essential way of behaving carries with it the implication that there is an *inessential* way of behaving and that the former has a value which is

---
[1] cf. pp. 20-24 & p. 28*ff*, above.

distinct from, and quite incommensurable with, the value (if any) which attaches to inessential behaviour. It is only upon this assumption that the ontological imperative could be understood as having any normative force. The moral version of the ontological imperative thus indicates the sole direction in which the value that attaches to our being as agents lies. This presents us with a question, viz. How are we to know what essential behaviour amounts to?

If we are to be able to act on the moral version of the ontological imperative ('Be what you essentially are') we must be able to determine—in a categorical fashion—what our essential mode of being is. It is crucial at this point to recognize that a *categorical* imperative cannot set forth a conception of what essential human behaviour amounts to if this conception has been derived from empirical considerations. It cannot be the result of a survey of which varieties of human endeavour are, in fact, the best. Such a derivation would involve the acceptance of some empirical criterion of value for human endeavour which would then have to be regarded as definitive of essential behaviour (and it is obvious that such an empirical investigation could not yield anything but a *hypothetical* imperative in any case). The very notion of determining an essence empirically (in effect, accepting that our essence is determined by empirical facts about us) is contrary to the logic of the word 'essence'. An essence is what makes a thing to be what it is: it defines a thing, not *vice versa*.

This means that, if the moral version of the ontological imperative ('Be what you essentially are') is to exhibit any categorical force, our way of knowing what we essentially are cannot be based on empirical observations of our behaviour. We must therefore be able to know *a priori* what the essential behaviour of a human agent should be. Our hypothesis, then, is that *everything* that contributes to the singular viability of the moral form of life follows from the logical fact that what essential human behaviour is *can only be determined a priori*. This is why the 'essential' version of the ontological imperative is to be regarded as the prototype of a moral injunction.

To illustrate: the familiar notion that a maxim must be universalizable if it is to be regarded as a categorical (and thus a moral) injunction stems from the need to have an *a priori* test for distinguishing *moral* maxims. I cannot determine *a priori* whether an individual's telling the truth or lying (on a given occasion) is right or wrong just by considering the facts about this particular case. Thus from 'If Peter were to lie...' nothing follows *a priori* except a tautology, viz. '...then he would have told a lie'. There is no logical recourse here for determining, *a priori*, the moral value of Peter's action. To determine this I must create the appropriate logical resources: I must universalize the situation ('If everyone were to lie...). When I do so, immediately the logic of the situation determines the practical inconsistency of such a universal practice. If everyone were to lie no one would be able to lie to any purpose, since lying, as a practice, is logically dependent on truth-telling being the normal practice.

So I find that the injunction applies to me, *a priori*, only if I regard myself as falling under the universal 'everyone'. If not, the logic will carry no weight with me. But how do I come to this conclusion *a priori*? Only by recognizing that, by definition (as a matter of logic), I, as a single individual (one of the 'ones' that the concept 'everyone' includes), necessarily feel the force of this universalized injunction. The only way that I can escape its force is not to think of the injunction as applying to me. But since if I reason at all, i.e. if I universalize my situation so that the internal logic of it can manifest itself (in Kant's phrase: if I have "enough conscience to ask" myself[2]), then I cannot avoid the consciousness that, as a rational being, I will be behaving inconsistently if I exempt myself from the rule that my own reasoning has revealed. I cannot *be* rational if I do not behave rationally, and since I *can* be rational (these very considerations are self-evidently the manifestation of my rationality) I must *behave* rationally—act in accordance with reason—*if I am to be what I essentially am*. This follows because, as Descartes argued, the process of determining my essence *a priori* reveals my essence. [Roughly: I cannot conceive of myself except as thinking therefore I am essentially a *thinking* thing[3]] And it then follows that behaving in accordance with what I essentially am must be one with behaving rationally. Why? Because to behave rationally is to behave in accordance with universalizable maxims, maxims which are valid (as guides to essential behaviour) because they are determined through *a priori* reasoning. Thus if I give any rational consideration at all to my behaviour (and to give no such consideration is to lapse into heteronomy, to become a mere phenomenon of nature) I must feel the force of my own reasoning. That is, I must recognize that it applies to me necessarily and thus stands with me as a categorical, a *moral*, consideration.

The force of the moral version of the ontological imperative is

---

[2] *FMM*, p. 81, BA 54.

[3] Descartes, René, Meditations on the first philosophy, Meditation II, in *The Philosophical works of Descartes*, translated by E.S. Haldane and G.R.T. Ross, Cambridge University Press, Cambridge, 1911, Vol. I, p.153

obligatory then upon any agent *in so far as it is rational*. Thus behaving rationally defines what behaving essentially (=morally), as opposed to inessentially, amounts to. It is clear that once the essential character of being human has been determined *a priori* (and has been found to lie with our capacity to reason *a priori*), the moral value (the value which comes from behaving in accordance with what you essentially are) which we then assign to human behaviour can only be a straightforward function of the fact that such behaviour has been guided by maxims which are valid *a priori*.

Now to review the situation: the moral version of the ontological imperative leads to a definition of a human being as a being which is what it is because it is capable of *a priori* reasoning and of directing its behaviour in accordance with that reasoning. This constitutes the essence to which the moral ontological imperative makes reference when it enjoins us to: 'Be what you essentially are'.

We noted that, in the original version of the ontological imperative (the tautological version 'Be what you are'), the injunction had no practical force. There is no sense in my saying that I am obliged to be what I am. I cannot *help* but be what I am. Now is it also the case that I cannot help being what I essentially am? If I am essentially a rational being could I behave in any other way? It would seem that the logic of the moral version of the ontological imperative dictates that I must be able to behave differently. But can I? Only, it would seem, by becoming something else—a being capable of inessential behaviour. So I must assume that I have (at least) two natures and that I can behave in accordance with either of them. One of these is my essential nature—I would not be what I am unless I were of this nature. The other is my inessential nature. Yet it seems I would not be what I am unless I could possess this nature as well, for otherwise the injunction 'Be what you essentially are' would collapse into a tautology so far as I am concerned. If it is to be intelligible to me as an injunction, I must normally exist in an inessential state, a state from which the idea of behaving essentially must appear as a *better* way of behaving. But in what sense 'better'? Since the value that attaches to behaving in accordance with what you essentially are is not an empirical value (it is not based on the evidence of people's actual preferences) it must be *self-evident* that behaving essentially is better than behaving inessentially.

It seems, then, as if 'essentially' is being used exhortatively, to point to an obviously better way of being. However, if this is the case, what are the grounds for considering it to be an obviously better way of being? There is, we believe, a 'self-evident' normative force which is implicit in the idea of being what you essentially are. This implicit force rests on certain fundamental contrasts between a thing's assuming its natural shape or achieving its natural end, and its being distorted or prevented from achieving its end. These normative contrasts take their normative force from the general idea of the harmonies or balances which result when each individual thing is allowed to function in such a way that it fits smoothly into the larger network of interactions reciprocally defining each individual's essential nature. There is, then, a deeply felt obviousness about the normative force of the moral version of the ontological imperative when it is thought of as being rooted in considerations of this sort. 'Be what you essentially are' amounts to an injunction to lead a life which allows you to assume your natural function and achieve your natural end.[4]

It is because of this obviousness that the consequences of behaving in defiance of moral laws commonly need no elaboration in order to demonstrate the wrongness of such behaviour. Thus the most common moral rebuke: 'What if everybody did that?' is taken to require no spelling out to explain its force. Because of this it can come to seem as if making an exception of oneself were wrong, period, without any consideration of what the consequences might be if everyone behaved in this way. It can come to seem to be a self-evident matter that making an exception of oneself (just by itself) is morally wrong.

Here we can clearly see how the *a priori* character of the moral form of life allows it to float free of empirical parameters of value, permitting it to create intrinsic *moral* value based on willing (in effect, thinking) in accordance with *a priori* considerations. One of the curiosities of the moral form of life which follows from its *a priori* origins is the fact that (logically) the value of moral behaviour has nothing to do with its empirical consequences. This means that moral behaviour itself is confined to a shadow activity, a 'willing' in accordance with moral maxims, an activity which is, in effect, no more than a mental affirmation or recognition of the rightness of the behaviour in question. Whether or not one's overt actions are in accordance with this recognition is a contingency which cannot affect the value created through the recognition of the rightness of the given maxim.[5] Let us now consider

---

[4] These considerations can be directly related to Kant's argument concerning the teleology of Reason discussed in Chapter Seven, pp. 101 ff.

[5] Indeed Kant (quite rightly) does not allow for the possibility of the

the agent-naturalistic version of the ontological imperative, viz. 'Be what you in fact are'.

We can start by considering the rather brash, but not unheard of response to the moral rebuke noted above ('What if everybody did that?'), viz. 'Everybody won't'. The rudeness of this remark and the fact that it is not easy to counter is rooted in the blunt refusal of the speaker to play the *a priori* game upon which the moral form of life is founded. The speaker does not accept the invitation to reason according to *a priori* rules, an invitation which is proffered by the word 'everybody' in the question: 'What if everybody did that?' Instead such speakers make a judgment, based on empirical considerations, that the consequences of their (personally) not following the rule will not be a universal shift in people's behaviour. They readily admit that, in general, people should behave in the manner which is suggested, but they reserve the right to judge, in any given case, whether such behaviour is warranted in this or that particular situation.

Thus their judgment of what warrants or does not warrant behaving in a 'moral' fashion is not based on *a priori* considerations but on something else, viz. a personal estimation—adequate or otherwise—of what the preferable course of action is. How can they know what is preferable? Only through experience. And how does experience deliver this knowledge? Simply in terms of the positive and negative feelings which they experience as a consequence of their actions when they see that they have judged wisely or foolishly. And it is the fact that people must *live* with these feelings that gives the agent-naturalistic version of the ontological imperative its authority. People experience responsibility for their judgments directly and inescapably in terms of their feelings. They thus have an immediate motive for tailoring their behaviour in line with the lessons which experience teaches them. The explicit assumption of this responsibility is effected through their recognition that their judgments are based on a *finite* span of past experience. In the light of this understanding of their fallibility, they acquire the *natural* moral responsibility which comes with recognizing that their duty lies in judging as deliberately as possible and learning from their mistakes. Everything connected with the morality (=wisdom) of their behaviour is

---

phenomenon of evil willing, a mental affirmation that formally denies the validity of a moral maxim. The validity of moral maxims is guaranteed *a priori* so that it is logically impossible to think (will) them to be invalid. Thus one could not lie solely for the sake of lying since lying, in itself, lacks the internal coherence which gives a practice (like truth-telling) its 'sake' i.e. its internal justification. Cf. *RWL*, pp. 30- 31, A 27-30 B 31-34.

Everything connected with the morality (=wisdom) of their behaviour is thus based on the acceptance of, first, the finitude of their judgment and, secondly, the fact of their being creatures with feelings who must, of necessity, live with the emotional consequences of their judgments. Understanding and accepting the nature of their responsibility as finite agents is the mark of maturity. On the agent-naturalistic view, it is the proper appreciation of these facts which constitutes dignity, for dignity is the quality displayed by people who have *accepted* the facts which determine the human condition and behave accordingly.

Now if the agent-naturalistic version of the ontological imperative is to be intelligible as a normative injunction we must assume that there is a state of being from which this injunction may be heard and heeded. This is a state in which the lessons of experience have produced firm habits of prudent reflection, but in which the injunction (to be what you in fact are) is only being followed implicitly. In this situation people are making judgments in the light of their experience, but not explicitly recognizing the actual character of the control they are exercising over their behaviour. However, once they do so—once they realize their situation as finite agents and the extent to which they are responsible for the control of their own behaviour—they can begin to obey the injunction consciously and thereby *take* responsibility for their judgments. At this point they can begin to navigate with a clearer vision of their own powers as agents. They can begin explicitly[6] to use their understanding of their capacities and thus begin to try to obey the agent-naturalist's injunction to be what they, in fact, are.

What then is the attraction of complying with the agent-naturalistic version of the ontological imperative? This is a difficult question because the recognition and the acceptance of the fact that we are finite, feeling agents does not seem to open up a new vista of behavioural possibilities that has anything like the romantic appeal of being moral. It lacks the aura which goes with being a person who lives according to moral principles and indeed would die for them. The agent-naturalist says only that we ought always to act with the clear recognition that our judgment is finite and that, whatever we do, we are going to have to live with the emotional consequences of our acts. So why should we obey this imperative? Here the agent-naturalist can make reference to the irresistible normative force of the original ontological imperative 'Be what you are': if we are—in fact—finite, feeling creatures, our only sane course is to recognize this fact and act accordingly. At this point the question of why

---

[6] See pp. 77 ff., above, for a discussion of the techniques which can be used when our understanding of our condition as agents is explicit.

we ought to obey the agent-naturalistic version of the ontological imperative becomes: 'What are the attractions of sane behaviour?' One would think that the answer to this question should be obvious, but Spinoza spells it out. He captures the attractiveness of the emotional state which characterizes sanity in his phrase *"acquiescentia in se ipso"*. This is the state in which we experience the "pleasure arising from a man's contemplation of himself and his own power of action".[7]

> Thus in life it is before all things useful to perfect the understanding or reason, as far as we can, and in this alone man's highest happiness or blessedness consists, indeed blessedness is nothing else but the contentment of spirit (*ipsa anima acquiescentia*), which arises from the intuitive knowledge of God: (*Ethics*, p. 237, IV Appendix IV.)

This understanding and acceptance of one's nature and one's place in Nature—for this is what "the intuitive knowledge of God" amounts to in this context—is a kind of liberation[8] (from any false, distorting conception of one's nature) and this is something to be enjoyed positively. Indeed it is much more enjoyable than its moral counterpart (self-contentment) which comes with the 'knowledge' that one has acted solely out of respect for a practically valid maxim. For in the moral case the prize can never actually be enjoyed with confidence: subreption is always a threat. But acquiescence of mind is a function of our appreciation of the fact that we are finite agents, a fact which is continually being corroborated by our experience of living and which can, therefore, be appreciated with ever-growing confidence:

> He who rightly realizes, that all things follow from the necessity of the divine nature, and come to pass in accordance with the eternal laws and rules of nature, will not find anything worthy of hatred, derision, or contempt, nor will he bestow pity on anything, but to the utmost extent of human virtue he will endeavour to do well, as the saying is, and to rejoice. (*Ethics*, p. 221, IV Proposition L Note.)

---

[7] *Ethics*, p. 178, II Definitions of Emotions XXV

[8] Spinoza's discussion of this liberation takes place in Book V of *The Ethics*, which is entitled: "Of Freedom". The freedom referred to is simply the freedom which comes with a proper understanding of the human condition. Our freedom as agents begins with the first inklings of our understanding of our powers and of our situation. As our understanding becomes steadlily more explicit our freedom manifests itself in the increasing sense of control, or attunement between thought and action, which this understanding confers upon our behaviour.

The agent-naturalistic version of the ontological imperative is a command to pursue this path, to do well and to rejoice through recognizing and accepting one's own abilities for what they are and through recognizing and accepting the fact that these abilities will necessarily be enhanced by harmonious interaction with other agents. It exhorts us to recognize this latter fact and to utilize these natural harmonies and so increase our powers of action.

Having said this much, it should be clear that the path which the injunction 'Be what you in fact are' exhorts us to follow is not an easy one. Given that our capacity to control ourselves is a variable capacity that depends on our understanding of our situation, there will be a conflict within us between the desire to increase the adequacy of our understanding (and so act with greater freedom = greater control) and the feeling that, as finite, we must resign ourselves to a standard of behaviour which will always fall short of what we could have done had we been able to understand our situation more adequately. We must, as it were, make peace with our finitude without ceasing to strive for ever greater adequacy of understanding.

The difficulties of the agent-naturalistic programme reduce to this simple fact: it is always up to us to discern whether we have done our best, given the situation and given our limited powers of understanding. And this is not easy. We often underestimate our abilities and hence set our expectations too low, or we cut our deliberations short (because they prove difficult) and let our unconsidered feelings serve for judgments. The result is a failure to fulfill our potential as agents, a failure to be what we in fact are, viz. finite agents with an infinite capacity for improvement.

To sum up: there are two principal drawbacks connected with the agent-naturalistic alternative to morality. The first is the fact that the delights of acquiescing in the human condition, of recognizing the limitations of human agency, are not immediately obvious when contrasted with the heroic possibilities which the moral form of life offers to us. Secondly, the burden of judgment which the agent-naturalistic path imposes is an uncomfortable one, since it imposes a responsibility on the individual which mechanistic naturalism does not. The responsibility of judging for ourselves can be readily evaded by interpreting our behaviour as no more than the result of causes over which we have no control. Naturalists, of necessity, follow the original exhortatory force) and cannot therefore, be said to be responsible, in any sense, for what they do. They are what they are.

The Basis of the Unique Viability of the Moral Form of Life

It should then be easy to see why it is that morality as a form of life takes root as strongly as it does, exhibiting a viability which is resistant to those agent-naturalistic characterizations of the human condition which seek to undermine it. For example, it is breathtakingly simple to explain why one ought to obey the moral law: you ought to simply because it is right to do so. Furthermore, it is a satisfying thing to do what is right; satisfying *in itself*. It is not a satisfaction which is always only 'more or less' satisfying as one's judgment matures: "What is required in accordance with the principle of autonomy of choice is easily and without hesitation seen by the commonest intelligence."[9] Moral satisfaction can be had without having to have made the monumental (and never-ending) struggle that is involved in acquiring the virtue of prudence. Morality gains enormously through simplifying the process of judging what you should do in a given situation. If people are not sure what to do they can simply consider what would happen if *everybody* did x or y and then behave accordingly, secure in the knowledge that what they are doing is right. Again, if people say 'But it won't matter if I do it', the moralist can say 'Who are you to make an exception of yourself? You have no right to make such a judgment. And furthermore, if you take it upon yourself to decide, you must take the responsibility for the consequences. However, if you follow Reason's dictates, whatever happens, you will have been right to have done so.' In short, the principal ground for the viability of the moral form of life is its simplicity (straightforward *a priori* reasoning gives you the rule to follow) and the certainty with which it bestows value ('rightness') upon our behaviour.

Morality works admirably then as a straightforward device for getting people to consider their actions as having reference to a set of values external to themselves. It provides a source of authority which remains unaffected by the interests of personal short-term desires and the imperfect wisdom of personal judgments. Adorned with these qualities it can serve as an ever present reminder that there is more to acting than reacting, that if one stops and thinks (in moralist terms, universalizes) a morally secure way of behaving will present itself. By contrast, the agent-naturalist's

---

[9] *CPrR*, p. 148, A 64.

way is not simple: there are no rules to follow other than the ones you produce through your own deliberations and there is no certainty that what you have done is right, since there is no independent standard of 'rightness' by which to test your judgment. Only the subsequent course of experience and your own feelings can serve to determine whether you have done well or badly and for a finite being mistakes must abound.

It would seem then that agent-naturalists, however convinced they might be of the falseness of morality, would not think of abandoning it as a technique for generating the kind of reflective response to experience that they espouse. In effect, they would value morality as an essential tool through which to develop the habit of reflection which will—in time—be seen as the means whereby they can begin to exercise their own judgment. And this would be done with a due appreciation of both the pitfalls of blind obedience to moral maxims and of the responsibility we are shouldering when we make up our own minds as to what we should do. Since prudence effectively constitutes wisdom for a finite creature and since moral injunctions are the universalized counsels of prudence, where we sense that our understanding of a given situation is not adequate, it will be wise (not 'right') to be guided by these precepts. An *appropriate* regard for the moral form of life is, then, an essential part of our *acquiescentia in se ipso*—our recognition and acceptance of our finitude.

I have thus completed all I wished to set forth touching the mind's power over the emotions and the mind's freedom. Whence it appears, how potent is the wise man, and how much he surpasses the ignorant man, who is driven only by his lusts. For the ignorant man is not only distracted in various ways by external causes without ever gaining the true acquiescence of his spirit, but moreover lives, as it were unwitting of himself, and of God, and of things, and as soon as he ceases to suffer, ceases also to be.

Whereas the wise man, in so far as he is regarded as such, is scarcely at all disturbed in spirit, but, being conscious of himself, and of God, and of things, by a certain eternal necessity, never ceases to be, but always possesses true acquiescence of his spirit.

If the way which I have pointed out as leading to this result seems exceedingly hard, it may nevertheless be discovered. Needs must it be hard, since it is so seldom found. How would it be possible, if salvation were ready to our hand, and could without great labour be found, that it should be by almost all men neglected? But all things excellent are as difficult as they are rare. (*Ethics*, pp. 270-271, V Proposition XLII Note.)

INDEX

Abbott, Thomas Kingsmill, 103n, 109n
absolute, xiv, 13, 44, 57, 59, 64, 67, 86 & n, 88, 91, 92, 98, 104, 109 & n, 114, 115n, 135-2, 141
active, 37, 47-9, 51-3, 71, 73, 78-80, 83, 84n, 88-9, 89, 93-4, 132, 145,
active absorption, 43
active/positive emotions, 79
active reflection, 43
acquiescence, xiv, 104, 134, 154, 155, 157
aesthetic judgments, 45, 84, 85-88, 88n
affects, 73, 80
agent causality, 91, 92-5
agent-naturalism/agent naturalist, xiv, 16n, 62n, 100, 101 & n, 108, 114, 127-8, 129-30, 131, 132, 133, 135, 140, 144-6,
agent-naturalistic (explanation), 90, 95, 98, 99-100, 108, 109, 114 & n , 116, 118n, 123n, 124, 125, 129-30, 136, 137, 140n, 141, 147, 152-57
Antinomy of practical reason, 6n, 7-14, 9n, 57n, 118
Aristotle, 9n, 102, 122n, 129, 7n
authority/authoritative, 14, 50-3, 56, 57-60, 61, 62, 114, 156
autonomy/autonomous, 18-19, 19n, 27, 29, 30, 38, 51, 55, 77, 111, 124n, 132-4, 156

Auxter, Thomas, 8n

Beck, Lewis White, 8n, 9n, 103n, 109n, 142n
Bentham, Jeremy, 17n
Beverluis, John, 8n
bondage, 78, 80, 81

Categorical, 48, 49n, 50, 51, 66, 67, 113n, 148-9
categorical imperative(s), 77, 88, 114, 130, 148
the Categorical Imperative, 5 & n, 48, 50, 60, 90, 98
categorical voice/persona of Reason, 22, 23, 28-9, 68
Categories, 84
Cavell, Stanley, 10n
certainty, 4 & n, 54, 55, 103, 105-6, 135-6, 146, 156
character, 32, 41
choice(s), 23, 27-9, 28n, 32n, 37, 38, 40, 41-2, 44, 47, 142 & n, 145-6, 156n
class-inclusion, 30n, 105
communitas, 65-66, 67
complement, 134-6
conscience, 21-34, 21n, 35, 40, 42, 64-7, 68, 104, 149
considered judgments, 46, 144
consistency/consistent, 23, 32-3, 46, 51 & n, 126
contentment, 4, 6, 73, 106, 107 & n, 120-1, 154, see also *self-*

159

contentment, true contentment
control, xiv, 27, 39, 56, 69, 71, 77-80, 84 & n, 85-6, 88-90, 91, 92, 94, control (con't.), 113n, 114 125, 128, 130, 132, 134, 137-8, 139, 144-5, 153, 155
Critique of Judgement, 84
Critique of Practical Reason, Second Critique, 17, 18, 87, 119
Critique of Pure Reason, 83

Danto, Arthur C., 69n
decision(s), 18, 29, 36, 37-8, 42, decision(s) (con't), 46-9, 52-3, 55-7, 58, 139, 142, 145-6
decision-making, 37, 41-3, 44, 46-8, 58, 68, 87n, see also *moral decision-making, natural decision-making, reflexive decision-making*
deliberation(s), 52, 126-7, 129, 146, 155, 157
delight, 84-5, 88, 107-8, 144, 155
Descartes, 149 & n
determination of the will, 108-10, 120-3,
determined, xiv, 18, 38n, 41-2, 69, 89-90, 94
determinism/deterministic, xiv, 13, 93
dignity, 16, 26&n, 27, 28, 45, 48, 49n, 50-1, 123-36, 153
dignity of others, 124 & n, 130-6,
disinterested, 45-6, 47, 52-3, 54n, 58-60, 96-8
dispositions/dispositional, 28, 56-8, 120, 129
dutiful, 23, 41-2, 86, 125
duty, xiii, 5-7, 8, 13, 14n, 16, 20, 21n, 23, 24-6 25n, 26n, 28n, 34, 49, 55, 67, 85-6, 88, 98-100, 104, 113n, 121, 124, 125n, 130, 132, 134-5, 144n, 152
Dusing, Klaus, 8n

emotion(s), 49n, 58, 61, 71, 78, 79, 80, 81, 97, 121-2, 157
emphatic metaphor, 57, 70 & n, 71
end(s), 6, 7, 14, 17, 45, 48, 93, 101, 102n, 107, 124, 130, 132, 151
end in itself, 6, 67, 86, 124
Epicureans, 120
essence, 75, 150
essential, 24, 32, 33, 40, 45, 77, 132n, 147-51, 157
esteem, 131
evil, 27-28
'explanation', 15, 16, 27
explicit (understanding), 36-7, 78, 79-80, 94, 99-101, 152, 153n, 155

faculties, 20, 42-3, 46n, 51, 85, 124
faculty, 13n, 18-19, 23, 25-6, 28, 83-4, 87, 100, 102n, 105, 106, 122-3
feeling(s), 1, 6, 7, 11, 12-3, 14, 16, 20, 28, 35, 38, 39, 46-7, 49n, 54, 61 &n, 62, 64, 84, 97, 108-12, 117-19, 121-3, 126-9, 131-2, 135, 140, 146, 152, 153, 157
felicific calculation/calculus, 17-18, 19, 21, 25-6
finite/finitude, xiv, 8, 48, 60 & n, 71-4, 76-8, 81, 86-7, 91, 93, 101 & n, 102, 103, 106, 108, 113 & n, 115-16, 117, 118n, 129, 130, 132 & n, 132-6, 137, 144, 152-4, 155, 156-7
first person (perspective), 31, 41-3,

first person (perspective), (con't), 60
flourishing, 89, 101 & n, 111, 134
free agent, 32, 39, 42, 52, 76, 88
free choice, 27, 28-30, 31, 33, 37, 38, 39, 40-2, 56-7, 68, 77n, 114, 146
free will, xiii, 39, 47, 49n, 52, 54, 77n, 92, 125, 137, 139 & n, 141-2
free exercise/act of the will, 18, 26-7, 35, 58, 63, 90
freedom, xiii, xiv, 2, 6n, 14n, 17, 26n, 27-34, 32n, 35, 36, 40, 41, 42, 48-57, 61, 64, 69, 75-6, 81, 111, 113-4, 120-1, 125 & n, 132, 136-46, 154, 155, 157
forbidden, 60

generosity, 141, 142
good, 4n, 7, 13, 23, 27-34, 37, 38 & n, 41, 61n, 74 & n, 76-7, 95-105, 118, 119-20, 131, 139-40, 143, 144-6, 156n, see also *highest good*
good in itself, 107
(the) good will, 5, 34, 95-102
goodness 29, 39

Hallett, H.F., xv (note), 69n
happiness, 1-2 & 2n, 4, 5 & n, 6-9 & 9n, 10-13, 14, 22, 24, 25, 28, 29, 36, 37, 38, 40, 45, 50, 54n, 63-8, 74-6, 99, 101, 103, 104, 106-8, 111, 116, 118-21, 123, 132-3
Harris, Errol, xv
harmonious/harmony, 33, 72-3, 75, 77, 85, 103-4, 132n, 132-5, 144, 155,
heterogeneity, 8-10, 119
heteronomy/heteronomous, 18, 19, 40, 51, 77, 139, 149
highest good, 8, 9 & n, 57n, 67, 118-9
Humanity-in-its-freedom, 26-33, 40-1, 42
humiliation/humiliate, 111, 118 & n
Hume, David, 45 & n, 59n, 87, 91, 100, 124-5, 131 & n, 142 & n
hypothetical, 18, 22, 45, 47-8, 113n, 148

ignorance, 76, 77 & n, 140 & n, 157
ill at ease/uneasiness, 36, 59 & n, 60, 131-2
imagination, 78, 85, 101, 132
imaginative projection, 4, 21n, 78
imperative: see *categorical imperative, moral imperative, ontological imperative*
implicit (understanding), 78, 79, 94, 99, 101, 151, 153
improving the understanding, 77-81
incentive, 49n, 108-11, 118, 123, 139, 142
inclination(s), 6n, 11, 15, 21, 24, 28 & n, 36, 37, 45, 50, 56, 58-9, 107n, 109-12, 121, 124, 126, 128, 134
inconsistency, 50-1, 148-9
indulgent, 28, 32, 33, 37, 38-9, 41-2
injunction, xiii, 4, 23, 26, 68, 148-51, 153, 155
inner life, 16, 21n, 25n
instinct, 2n, 45, 102-3
intelligible Author of Nature, 10
interaction, 65, 71-3, 132-5, 144, 151, 155
interest(s), 23, 31, 40, 58, 87, 97, 99, 128, 131, 146, 156
intrinsic, 87, 95, 123, 125-6, 129, 133, 135, 141-2, 145, 151
intuition/intuitive, 70-1, 133-5, 144,

161

intuition/intuitive, (con't), 151, 155

joy, 61n, 73-4 & n, 76, 123, 134-5
judgment, 22n, 38 & n, 45-7, 52 & n, 58-60, 75, 84-5, 105, 111, 112-3, & n, 114 & n, 128, 138, 144-5, 153, 153, 155-6, 157: see also *considered judgments, moral judgment(s)*.
judgmental feelings, 38, 39, 46, 49 & n, 50, 51-3, 54n, 55-62, 59n, 63, 68, 107, 137n, 146

kindness, 141-5, 146

language-game, 14-15, 117, 137
legality, 25n, 49,
liberation, 154 & n

maxim(s), 2n, 3 & n, 4-6, 5n, 9, 11n, 21, 22-3, 24, 26-7, 30-1, 46, 51, 60-1, 65, 79, 88, 108, 111-2, 115, 116-121, 127, 130, 148-9, 151-52 & n, 154, 157
mechanical/mechanistic, xiv, 62n, 93, 155
Milton's Satan, 29
mitigation/mitigated agency, 71-2, 73, 79, 115, 134
Montaigne, 107
moral causality, 17-34, 35, 54, 109: see also: *natural causality*
moral decision-making, 38, 44, 47, 55-6, 68
moral law, 4n, 5, 6, 13 & n, 14, 19n, 25n, 49n, 62, 87, 108, 109-10 109n, 118n, 124-7, 130, 134, 137, 139, 140-1, 142n, 143, 145-6, 151
moral precepts, 68, 99

moral imperatives, 48, 147
moral judgment(s), 58, 60, 76-7
moral obligation, 39
moral value, 1-2, 2n, 3, 5-7, 9-10, 13, 15, 16, 20, 25-7, 32, 37, 39, 40-1, 42, 44-9, 49, 51 & n, 54, 55, 58, 62, 63, 65-6, 67, 68, 86-90, 102, 132-3, 139-43, 150-1, cf. *natural value, utility value*
moralism/moralist, 77, 100, 125-7, 130, 132-5, 141-2, 144-6, 157
motive(s), 13, 14, 67, 71, 110, 122-5, 132, 139: see also *natural motives*
motivation/motivated/motivational, 8, 13, 17, 18, 20, 21-3, 25-6, 28, 32, 34, 49-52, 49n, 53, 55-59, 61, 62, 67, 79, 86, 100, 109-10, 118-9, 121-2, 125-6, 146
Murphy, Jeffrie G., 8n
mutual satisfaction, 107, 134-5
mutual trust, 66, 67-8, 99
mystery/mysterious, 34, 49, 50, 52, 64, 76, 92, 139, 138, 140, 141, 143

natural account/explanation, xiv, 15-16, 18, 19, 99-100, 140, 143
natural causality, 14-16, 17, 19, 21, 34, 37, 54, 57
natural decision-making, 44, 68
natural morality, 62
natural motive(s), 23, 53, 56, 100, 123
natural value, 10, 16, 31, 45, 66, 98, 141-2, 144
natural(istic) account/explanation, 42, 45, 64, 91-2, 124, 131, 132
negative satisfaction, 6n, 7, 11, 66n, 120
neutral perspective, 39, 56, 61-2

obedience, 112, 115, 157
obligation, 14 & n, 16, 20, 23, 27, 49, 51, 52, 108, 114, 143
on principle, 26-7, 33-4, 64-5, 99-100, 107 & n
ontological, 23, 29, 32, 33-35, 38, 42, 52n, 56n, 64, 137, 153-9
ontological commitment, 29-31
ontological imperative, 23n, 29, 32, 128, 147-8
ontological principle, 32
ontological value(s), 30
original model (of natural causality), 18, 19, 21-2, 34
ought, xiii, 14 & n, 25n, 29, 32, 43-4, 48, 52, 113, 147, 156
ought implies can, xiii, xv, 14, 113, 137

pain, 21, 61n, 73, 79
Pasotti, R., 61n
passive, 36, 38n, 42, 47-8, 71-2, 90, 92, 93-4, 122, 126, 128-9, 145
passive absorption, 43
passive/negative emotion(s), 79,
passive reflection, 44, 57, 58, 61-2
passive reflexive consciousness, 44-6, 47, 48, 52-3, 55-6, 57, 58-9, 61-2, 68
passive spectator, 42
perfection, 73
permissible/permitted, 4, 33-4, 45-6, 60
personal gain, 143-4
personification/personified, 23n, 23-31, 40, 46n, 50, 62
perspective/point of view, 46, 59, 74, 76, 118n see also *neutral perspective, sense of perspective, spectator perspective, first person (perspective), third person (perspective)*
pleasure, 21, 34, 73, 75, 85, 122, 154
postulate(s), xiii, 26n
practical validity, 3-5, 21, 22-4, 26-8, 30-34, 45, 47, 60-1, 65, 66, 68, 104, 115-6
precept(s), 79, 80, 157
pre-cognition, 138
predispositions/predisposed, 28, 37, 40
preference(s)/preferring, 27-9, 37, 50, 146, 150, 152
price, 27, 89, 124, 129, 134
principle(s), 3n, 4n, 18, 32-4, 37, 40-1, 61, 99-100, 111, 141, 143, 153, 156 see also *on principle, ontological principle*
principle of indulgence, 32
prudence/prudential, 1-2, 1n, 2n, 4-5, 9, 21, 28, 34, 67-8, 86, 99-101, 104, 106, 108, 153, 156, 157
pure, 6, 22, 31, 38n, 47, 58, 66, 80, 84-5, 88, 90, 123, 143-4
Pure Concepts of the Understanding, 84
ratio cognoscendi, 14n, 98
ratio essendi, 26n

rational, 5, 8-10, 9n, 10n, 18, 22-4, 27, 28-9, 32-3, 40, 48-50, 51, 55, 75, 99, 102, 107-9, 117, 124, 126-7, 129-31, 149-50
rational willing, 33, 62
reason; 'How can reason be practical?', 13, 15-16, 17, 18-20, 23-4, 35, 54-5
reason's dictates, 14, 29, 34, 39, 49, 51, 53-4, 57, 102, 108, 156

reasoning, 17, 22, 30 & n, 45, 48, 51-2, 74, 70-76, 102, 105-6, 111, 149, 150
reciprocity/reciprocal, 72-3, 76, 98-9, 102-3, 132n, 134, 151
reflection, 38, 39, 47, 53, 58, 60, 149, 153, 157
reflexive awareness, 23, 39-62, 126-30
reflexive self, 39, 41-2
reflexive decision-making, 35-62
relationship, 30n, 99, 103-4, 105, 126
respect, 1, 16, 33, 49, 109n, 113n, 117n, 125, 132, 133, 135, 143
respect for the moral law, 55, 108-18, 121, 134, 137, 139, 140-1, 143-4
responsibility/responsible, 14, 19, 27&n, 56, 87, 92, 111-5, 112n, 114n, 130, 144-5
rules, 11n, 17&n, 30n, 51, 65, 85, 86n, 87 & n, 88, 99, 101, 106 & n, 107-8, 114-16, 132, 144, 149, 152, 154

salvation, 79, 157
sanity, 145, 153-4
satisfaction(s), 2n, 6-7, 13, 15, 18, 19, 20-1 22, 24-5, 27, 28, 29, 33, 44, 54, 62, 63-4, 66, 67-8, 93, 106, 156: see also *mutual satisfaction, negative satisfaction, true satisfaction*
self-centred, 104, 118
self-conceit, 111, 117n, 118n
self-contentment, 6-8, 10-12 & 12n, 16, 25, 27, 29, 34, 36, 54 & n, 60, 63-4, 89, 118, 134, 154
self-interest, 1n, 45, 124-5

self-respect, 26n, 28, 127, 129, 133
sense of perspective, 128,
shadow language-game, 15
shadow model (of moral causality), 14-16, 17-34, 35, 109
Shahan, Robert W., xv
shame, 126-30
Silber, John R., 5n, 8n, 14n
spectator perspective, 46, 56-7, 62
spectator self, 56, 61
spontaneity/spontaneous, 30 & n, 31, 69, 83-5, 88, 136-46, 139n, 141, 142n
Stoics, 118-9
subjective maxim, 49-50
subreption/subreptive influence, 47, 53, 68, 122, 143, 146n, 154
subsumption, 105
superimposition/superimpose, 44, 54, 55, 62, 68, 130, 139, 147
supernatural/supernaturalism, xiv, 92-4, 125 & n, 138
syllogism, 30n, 87n

technique(s), 77, 78-80, 88, 128 & n, 138, 139 & n, 157
teleology of Reason, 2n, 103-8, 151
third person (perspective), 41-2, 44, 45, 53, 50, 62
transcendental, 9n, 26, 83-4
Treatise of Human Nature, A, 45n, 100n, 107n, 124 & n, 131n, 142n
true contentment, 104
true satisfaction, 117
true to oneself, 23, 38, 61-2
trust, 3, 38, 65-7, 99, 101

ulterior motives, 13, 26, 139
unconditional value, 2, 6, 12, 67,

unconditional value, (con't), 96-99, 107-110
universal(ity), 4, 5n, 24, 46, 59, 65-6, 68, 96, 104, 109n, 112, 115-18, 125-27, 148-9, 152
universalize/universalizable, 3-4, 5n, 30n, 31, 64-5, 148-9, 157
utilitarian, 85, 87, 116, 118, 124-5, 144 & n
utility value, 1-2, 2n, 4-5, 12-13, 46-7, 63, 64, 65-6, 67, 95-6, 142

validity, 30n, 108, 109, 114, 116, 118, 126, 127, 151
valuable in itself, 95, 97-8
viable/viability, 36, 39, 52, 54, 59-60, 61, 62
virtue, 7-8 & n, 9&n, 10-11, 12, 13n, 52, 63-4, 118-122, 131, 154, 156

virtus noumenon, 42
virtus phaenomenon, 42

well-being, 2n, 4n, 36, 39, 45, 54n, 59-60, 66-7
will(ing), 4n, 9, 10, 15n, 16, 22-34, 24n, 37, 39, 41, 54-5, 60n, 74 & n, 75, 76, 80, 81 & n, 92, 93-101, 105, 106, 112, 119, 135, 138, 139-42, 142n, 151 see also *rational willing*
will-power, 81,
wisdom, wise, 21, 103, 108, 111-12, 114n, 118n, 152, 156, 157
Wittgenstein, L., 14

Zelden, Mary-Barbara, 8n

David E. Ward was born in Toronto, Canada, and is a Senior Lecturer in the Philosophy Department of the University of Otago, Dunedin, New Zealand.

Robyn McPhail was born in Gore, New Zealand, and was until 1987 a tutor in the Philosophy Department of the University of Otago. She is now a Presbyterian Minister with the Alexandra-Clyde-Lauder Union Parish in Central Otago, New Zealand